AF835103

Stephen Knight and Margo Munro Kerr are barristers at One Pump Court Chambers specialising in crime, immigration, and public law. Much of their work is focussed on how the intersection of these areas of law can assist victims of trafficking to escape and recover from the further oppression they suffer as a result of the actions of the British state and legal system.

Victims of Trafficking: A Practical Guide to Criminal Defence and Appeals

Victims of Trafficking: A Practical Guide to Criminal Defence and Appeals

Stephen Knight

Margo Munro Kerr

Law Brief Publishing

Published 2026 by Law Brief Publishing, an imprint of Law Brief Publishing Ltd
30 The Parks
Minehead
Somerset
TA24 8BT

www.lawbriefpublishing.com

Paperback: 978-1-918241-20-4

To our clients, and to our colleagues, seeking justice.

PREFACE

Two days before he is due to be deported, a Vietnamese man in Brook House Immigration Removal Centre finally manages to speak to an immigration lawyer. He has a conviction for cultivating cannabis which led to a two-year prison sentence. After a year inside, the halfway point when most British citizens would be released, he was detained under immigration powers. To challenge his deportation, an immigration lawyer will have to show why it would breach his human rights to be returned to Vietnam. He's extremely traumatised and he's also autistic, making it very hard to take instructions from him quickly enough. He might end up back in Vietnam without his immigration case ever being heard.

A Kurdish woman pleaded guilty to an immigration offence when the judge told her she would be released that day with time served. The Home Office later agreed she would face persecution from the Turkish state but says that she doesn't qualify for asylum because of her conviction. As a result, the Home Office only grants her 30 months' discretionary leave to remain. She may never be eligible for indefinite leave to remain or citizenship in the UK. After 29 months she applies to renew her discretionary leave, but she doesn't hear back for 18 months, during which time she becomes homeless because she cannot prove to anyone that she has the right to live in the UK, to work, or to obtain benefits.

A British child convicted of a robbery when he was 13 is now being prosecuted for robbery again aged 15. There is a Single Competent Authority decision stating that at the time of the recent robbery, on the balance of probabilities, he was a victim of trafficking. But the Crown Prosecution Service, in weighing up the factors in favour of prosecution and the factors against, take into account his previous conviction. They decide to continue prosecuting him, in part because of his previous offence. The defence object on the basis that he was also a victim of trafficking at age 13 and so the previous robbery conviction should not weigh in favour of prosecution. Legal arguments follow, but because a further decision from the Single Competent Authority is needed, he has been on bail for this offence for 18 months. During this time he has been excluded from school because of the ongoing proceedings. He's more vulnerable to trafficking than ever. And he's now almost 18 years old, which means that if he is convicted and sentenced, he'll likely be supervised by adult probation.

These people all could have been successfully defended if the right approaches had been used to their cases. They now all have convictions for offences which they committed as a result of exploitation. Those convictions are part of the web of borders and prisons which is making their lives miserable. They may all have a way to appeal their convictions, which might go some way to untangling the web.

A criminal conviction is harmful to anyone, even beyond sentence. A person with a previous conviction is more likely to be arrested and charged again. The conviction could be used against them at trial. If found guilty, their chances of staying out of prison will be lower, and their sentence will likely be longer than for a person without a previous conviction. But people who have experienced trafficking are particularly likely to suffer complex harms as a result of conviction. They are more likely to fall back into criminality, either through being re-trafficked, or through being marginalised and without support (the same reasons they were vulnerable to trafficking in the first place). For non-British citizens, a conviction could lead to deportation. Even if they are not deported, they could still be excluded from permanent status, which means that for months and even years on end they will be in limbo whenever they try to renew their status, facing an uncertain future and difficulties working, renting a home, or accessing benefits.

For those reasons, practitioners should be alert to how to defend potential victims of trafficking, and to the possibility of appealing convictions arising out of human trafficking, even years after those convictions occur. The law set out in this book explains how to mount such a defence, and a route to appeal. This area of law has changed rapidly over the last decade.

With the Modern Slavery Act 2015, a specific defence was created for some victims of trafficking accused of criminal offences. Cases which followed the Modern Slavery Act confirmed that the state still has a duty not to prosecute victims of trafficking in certain circumstances, notwithstanding the availability of a statutory defence in some cases. More recently it has been confirmed that this remains the case even where a defendant has pleaded guilty. As a result, there may be merit to an appeal against conviction where a potential appellant has been recognised to be a victim of trafficking after being convicted of an offence.

We hope that this short book explaining the recent legal developments, and grounded in practice, will be helpful to others who, like ourselves, are interested in defending victims of trafficking and appealing against their convictions.

We begin in Part 1 with sections defining trafficking and setting out the obligations towards victims of trafficking. Some – particularly the obligation not to prosecute and punish victims of trafficking – may seem obviously relevant to a book about criminal defence and appeals. Others – such as the obligation to grant reflection and recovery periods – may appear less relevant. We deal with them to contextualise the non-liability obligations, and also because the other obligations included in the book may have some bearing on the problems faced by people who have been criminalised, and so legal practitioners in the field should be aware of them in order to know when an individual could be referred for further support elsewhere.

In Part 2 we then deal with the way that a victim of trafficking will proceed through the criminal legal system up to and including trial, and strategies that are relevant in their defence. Even if the reader is interested only in the question of appeals, it is necessary to understand these issues in order to understand how appeals operate.

Part 3 of this book turns to the substance of appeals in trafficking cases. We deal firstly with appeals against conviction, then against sentence, and then some matters relevant to all appeals. This part of the book is informed by the material that has gone before it: anyone undertaking an appeal in a trafficking case will need to have a full understanding of how obligations towards victims of trafficking arise, and how they are meant to prevent convictions, in order to understand what needs to be done when victims of trafficking have been failed by the criminal legal system.

The book ends with a conclusion dealing with ancillary matters that lawyers should think about when undertaking trafficking appeals, such as civil matters that may arise out of the state's inadequate response to victims of trafficking. This element of the book cannot be comprehensive, but should provide practitioners with a starting point to consider wider issues.

The content of this book is aimed primarily at criminal defence lawyers. The intention is that it will be an easily accessible guide to support appeals in trafficking cases. We therefore set out directions where the law could be taken, and litigation strategies that may be effective. However, we have attempted not to be overconfident in our exploration of such future directions and strategies: it would benefit no one for us to do so.

We encourage readers to integrate the arguments in this book into their practice. If practitioners find parts of our text helpful then they can be used in skeleton arguments or written pleadings.

We are immensely grateful to our colleague Professor Parosha Chandran for her invaluable comments on a draft of this text. Any errors remain our own.

The law within this book is up to date to the time of writing, on 29 January 2026.

Stephen Knight
Margo Munro Kerr
One Pump Court Chambers
March 2026

CONTENTS

TABLE OF CASES

AAC, R v [2023] EWCA Crim 15

AAD, AAH, and AAI, R v [2022] EWCA Crim 106, [2022] 1 WLR 4042

Abdul-Hussain (Mustafa Shakir), R v [1998] EWCA Crim 3528

AFU, R v [2023] EWCA Crim 23

Ahluwalia, R v (1993) 96 Cr App R 133

Antar, R v [2004] EWCA Crim 2708

Asiedu, R v [2015] EWCA Crim 714, [2015] 2 Cr App R 8

AUL, R v [2022] EWCA Crim 1435

Baniulyte, R v [2025] EWCA Crim 1205

BLS, R v [2022] EWCA Crim 1079

BNN, R v [2024] EWCA Crim 991

Boal, R v [1992] QB 591

Bowen, R v [1997] 1 WLR 372

Brandford, R v [2016] EWCA Crim 1794, [2017] 4 WLR 17

Brecani, R v [2021] EWCA Crim 731, [2021] 1 WLR 5851

BRP, R v [2023] EWCA Crim 40

BSG, R v [2023] EWCA Crim 1041

BXR, R v [2022] EWCA Crim 1483

BYA, R v [2022] EWCA Crim 1326

CS, Le, R v [2021] EWCA Crim 134

Dastjerdi (Bakhshi Ali), R v [2011] EWCA Crim 365

Dumitru Palazu, R v [2020] EWCA Crim 1627

Fortean, R v [2009] EWCA Crim 437

Foster, R v [1985] QB 115

Frost-Helmsing (Anthony), R [2010] EWCA Crim 1200

Ginar (Aydin), R v [2023] EWCA Crim 1121, [2024] 1 WLR 1264

Grant-Murray, R v [2017] EWCA Crim 1228

Gray, R v [2014] EWCA Crim 2372, [2015] 1 Cr App R (S) 27

GS, R v [2018] EWCA Crim 1824, [2019] 1 Cr App R 7

GS v United Kingdom (no 7604/19)

James, R v [2018] EWCA Crim 285, [2018] 1 WLR 2749

Johnson (Jennifer Nancy), R v [2022] EWCA Crim 832

King, R v [2000] 2 Cr App R 391

Kirk, R v [2015] EWCA Crim 1764

L & N, R v [2017] EWCA Crim 2129

Makuwa, R v [2006] EWCA Crim 175, [2006] 1 WLR 2755

Martin, R v (1989) 88 Cr App R 343

Mateta, R v [2013] EWCA Crim 1372, [2014] 1 WLR 1516

McCook, R v [2014] EWCA Crim 734, [2016] 2 Cr App R 30

MK, Gega, R v [2018] EWCA Crim 667, [2019] QB 86

Monnell and Morris v United Kingdom (nos 9562/81 and 9818/82) (1988) 10 EHRR 205

N, R v [2019] EWCA Crim 984

Nea Karteria Maritime Co v Atlantic and Great Lakes Steamship Corp (No2) [1981] Com LR 138

Nightingale, R v [2013] EWCA Crim 405, [2013] 2 Cr App R 7

O, R v [2019] EWCA Crim 1389

Ortiz, R v (1986) 83 Cr App R 173

Owusu Yianoma v Bar Standards Board [2023] EWHC 2785 (Admin)

Phillips v Isleworth Crown Court [2023] EWHC 617 (Admin), [2023] 2 Cr App R 8

Practice Note (CA: Crime: Applications for Leave to Appeal) [1970] 1 WLR 663

R (on the application of ABW) v Secretary of State for the Home Department [2025] EWHC 3280 (Admin)

R (on the application of FH) v Secretary of State for the Home Department [2024] EWHC 1327 (Admin)

R (on the application of Golrokhi) v Chelmsford Crown Court [2013] EWHC 4343 (Admin)

R (on the application of Hoar-Stevens) v Richmond upon Thames Magistrates' Court [2003] EWHC 2660 (Admin)

R (on the application of O and H) v Secretary of State for the Home Department [2019] EWHC 148 (Admin)

R (on the application of TDT) v Secretary of State for the Home Department [2018] EWCA Civ 1395, [2018] 1 WLR 4922

R (on the application of the Crown Prosecution Service) v Crown Court at Preston [2023] EWHC 1957 (Admin), [2024] KB 348

R v Blandford Justices ex parte G [1967] 1 QB 82

R v Durham Quarter Sessions ex parte Virgo [1952] 2 QB 1

Rantsev v Cyprus and Russia (no 25965/04) (2010) 51 EHRR 1

Sadighpour, R v [2012] EWCA Crim 2669, [2013] 1 WLR 2725

Siliadin v France (no 73316/01) (2006) 43 EHRR 16

Singh (Kunwar), R v [2017] EWCA Crim 466, [2018] 1 WLR 1425

SM v Croatia (no 60561/14) (2021) 72 EHRR 1

Swain, R v [1986] Crim LR 480

Tredget, R v [2022] EWCA Crim 108, [2022] 4 WLR 62

TV v Spain (no 22512/21) [2025] Crim LR 96

Van der Mussele v Belgium (no 8919/80) (1984) 6 EHRR 163

VCL and AN v The United Kingdom (nos 77587/12 and 74603/12) (2021) 73 EHRR 9

Verney, R v (1909) 2 Cr App R 107

VSJ, R v [2017] EWCA Crim 36, [2017] 1 WLR 3153

Webb & Somerset-How, R v [2025] EWCA Crim 1491

Wilson, R v [2016] EWCA Crim 65

TABLE OF STATUTES

Commission Decision of 14 October 2011 on the request by the United Kingdom to accept Directive 2011/36/EU of the European Parliament and of the Council on preventing and combating trafficking in human beings and protecting its victims, and replacing Council Framework Decision 2002/629/JHA (notified under document C(2011) 7228)

Convention for the Protection of Human Rights and Fundamental Freedoms 1950

Convention Relating to the Status of Refugees 1951

Council of Europe Convention on Action against Trafficking in Human Beings 2005 (Council of Europe Treaty Series - No 197)

Criminal Appeal Act 1968

Criminal Appeal Act 1995

Criminal Practice Directions 2023

Criminal Procedure Rules, SI 2025/909

Directive 2011/36/EU of the European Parliament and of the Council of 5 April 2011 on preventing and combating trafficking in human beings and protecting its victims, and replacing Council Framework Decision 2002/629/JHA 2011

Directive (EU) 2024/1712 of the European Parliament and of the Council of 13 June 2024 amending Directive 2011/36/EU on preventing and combating trafficking in human beings and protecting its victims 2024

Modern Slavery Act 2015

Prosecution of Offences Act 1985

Protocol to Prevent, Suppress and Punish Trafficking in Persons Especially Women and Children, supplementing the United Nations Convention against Transnational Organized Crime 2000

Sentencing Children and Young People Guideline

TABLE OF SECONDARY MATERIALS

Bar Mutual Indemnity Fund, '2025 Terms of Cover'

Committee on the Rights of the Child, 'General Comment No. 24 (2019) on Children's Rights in the Child Justice System' (United Nations 2019) CRC/C/GC/24

Council of Europe, 'Chart of Signatures and Ratifications of Treaty 197' (*Treaty Office*, 7 February 2022) <https://www.coe.int/en/web/conventions/full-list> accessed 7 February 2022

Criminal Cases Review Commission, 'Casework Policy: Exceptional Circumstances CW-POL-06'

'Crown Court Compendium Part I - October 2025'

Crown Prosecution Service, 'Modern Slavery, Human Trafficking and Smuggling' (*The National Archives*, 22 January 2022) <https://webarchive.nationalarchives.gov.uk/ukgwa/20220122231648/https:/www.cps.gov.uk/legal-guidance/modern-slavery-human-trafficking-and-smuggling> accessed 30 December 2025

——, 'Immigration' (13 February 2024) <https://www.cps.gov.uk/prosecution-guidance/immigration> accessed 12 December 2025

——, 'Costs - Annex 1' (30 April 2024) <https://www.cps.gov.uk/prosecution-guidance/costs-annex-1> accessed 12 December 2025

——, 'Modern Slavery and Human Trafficking: Offences and Defences, Including the Section 45 Defence' (22 July 2025) <https://www.cps.gov.uk/prosecution-guidance/modern-slavery-and-human-trafficking-offences-and-defences-including-section> accessed 11 December 2025

'Director's Guidance on Charging' (December 2020) <https://www.cps.gov.uk/prosecution-guidance/directors-guidance-charging-sixth-edition-december-2020-incorporating-national> accessed 11 December 2025

'Guide to Proceedings in the Court of Appeal, Criminal Division'

Home Office, 'Victims of Modern Slavery: Competent Authority Guidance, Version 8.0'

'Modern Slavery: National Referral Mechanism and Duty to Notify Statistics UK, Quarter 2 2025 - April to June' (*GOV.UK*) <https://www.gov.uk/government/statistics/modern-slavery-nrm-and-dtn-statistics-april-to-june-2025/modern-slavery-national-referral-mechanism-and-duty-to-notify-statistics-uk-quarter-2-2025-april-to-june> accessed 11 December 2025

'Modern Slavery: National Referral Mechanism and Duty to Notify Statistics UK, Quarter 3 2025 - July to September' (*GOV.UK*) <https://www.gov.uk/government/statistics/modern-slavery-nrm-and-dtn-statistics-july-to-september-2025/modern-slavery-national-referral-mechanism-and-duty-to-notify-statistics-uk-quarter-3-2025-july-to-september> accessed 11 December 2025

'Modern Slavery: Statutory Guidance for England and Wales (under S49 of the Modern Slavery Act 2015) and Non-Statutory Guidance for Scotland and Northern Ireland (Accessible Version)' (*GOV.UK*, 24 December 2025) <https://www.gov.uk/government/publications/modern-slavery-how-to-identify-and-support-victims/modern-slavery-statutory-guidance-for-england-and-wales-under-s49-of-the-modern-slavery-act-2015-and-non-statutory-guidance-for-scotland-and-northe> accessed 29 December 2025

'National Referral Mechanism Guidance: Adult (England and Wales)' (*GOV.UK*) <https://www.gov.uk/government/publications/human-trafficking-victims-referral-and-assessment-forms/guidance-on-the-

national-referral-mechanism-for-potential-adult-victims-of-modern-slavery-england-and-wales> accessed 11 December 2025

Office of the Special Representative and Co-ordinator for Combating Trafficking in Human Beings, 'Policy and Legislative Recommendations towards the Effective Implementation of the Non-Punishment Provision with Regard to Victims of Trafficking' (Organization for Security and Co-operation in Europe (OSCE) 2013)

Rawlinson K, 'Prosecutors Target Smuggled People Who Were Forced to Pilot Small Boats' (*The Guardian*, 23 February 2024) <https://www.theguardian.com/world/2024/feb/23/people-smuggling-gangs-small-boats-home-office-migration> accessed 11 December 2025

United Nations, 'United Nations Treaty Collection' (*United Nations Treaty Collection*, 8 April 2022) <https://treaties.un.org/pages/ViewDetails.aspx?src=TREATY&mtdsg_no=XVIII-12-a&chapter=18&clang=_en> accessed 8 April 2022

United Nations Office on Drugs and Crime, 'Travaux Préparatoires of the Negotiations for the Elaboration of the United Nations Convention against Transnational Organized Crime and the Protocols Thereto' (United Nations 2006)

Working Group on Trafficking in Persons, 'Report on the Meeting of the Working Group on Trafficking in Persons Held in Vienna on 14 and 15 April 2009' (Conference of the Parties to the United Nations Convention against Transnational Organized Crime 2009) CTOC/COP/WG.4/2009/2

——, 'Report on the Meeting of the Working Group on Trafficking in Persons Held in Vienna from 27 to 29 January 2010' (Conference of the Parties to the United Nations Convention against Transnational Organized Crime 2010) CTOC/COP/WG.4/2010/6

PART ONE

AN OVERVIEW OF TRAFFICKING

CHAPTER ONE

THE DEFINITION OF HUMAN TRAFFICKING

Introduction: The United Kingdom's freely-chosen international obligations

Understanding who is a victim of trafficking first requires an understanding of what human trafficking is. As with much of the law in this area, a full understanding of the definitions requires looking outside the United Kingdom's domestic law, to a series of international agreements and soft law instruments. These international legal materials have become binding on the United Kingdom through domestic legislation based on them, the caselaw of the European Court of Human Rights, and the United Kingdom's own freely chosen international obligations.

The United Kingdom has chosen to accede to a series of international agreements relating to the prevention of trafficking in human beings, and the protection of victims of human trafficking. These international agreements have progressively increased the protections to which victims of modern slavery and human trafficking are entitled. They have also gradually led to an international consensus that victims of trafficking have a right to non-punishment for some otherwise criminal acts or omissions which are linked to their trafficking. This international consensus has been progressively evolving for over 25 years.

While this book is directed at practitioners within the English criminal legal system, the non-punishment principle derives from the United Kingdom's international legal obligations, which inform and, where necessary, extend beyond domestic statutory and procedural provisions. The analytical direction needs to remain clear: international law defines the scope of the relevant principles; domestic law must conform to that scope in international law, not limit it. The practical task in this area is not to fall into the limits of domestic law when applying principles which originate outside it. Concepts around trafficking law are autonomous legal concepts with autonomous meanings, which may differ from those which are normally seen in domestic law. Domestic law has so far accommodated the principles derived from international law only in part, but must be interpreted in light of the international legal principles.

As such, the law applicable in the United Kingdom must now be made to reflect the non-punishment principle contained in international legal obligations, even if that law is often poorly understood and inconsistently applied in practice. When courts consider arguments regarding non-punishment of victims of trafficking, it must always be borne in mind that the right to non-punishment is neither novel nor optional, but is well-established and binding law based on international commitments to which the United Kingdom has freely consented.

The principle of non-punishment has also been described as non-liability or non-criminalisation. It requires that victims of trafficking are not held liable for unlawful acts committed as a direct consequence of their trafficking. This encompasses protection from prosecution and from punishment (i.e. penalisation), as well as from other punitive measures.

The importance of the right not to be subject to penalties in the criminal legal system is obvious: the domestic courts have held that where a person's agency has been subverted, their culpability for offending linked to their trafficking may be reduced to the extent that it would be inappropriate to punish them. In such circumstances, instead of being criminalised, victims of modern slavery or human trafficking should be assisted to reflect and recover.

It is worth noting that the international consensus is that the non-punishment principle is not a mere principle of mitigation: it is a protection against liability itself. Therefore, victims should not merely receive reduced sentences, but should not be subject to liability.

The importance of non-prosecution is of equal importance: if a person is subject to a prosecution process then they are unable to reflect and recover, and will be subjected to further trauma by the prosecution. The prosecution process itself often entails both a loss of liberty through being remanded in custody, and a fear of further ill-treatment by the state which may result in further traumatisation. As such, when states prosecute victims of trafficking or subject them to criminal penalties they perpetuate the harm of trafficking further, rather than preventing it. Not only may this be seen as morally wrong, but it also obstructs the United Kingdom's ability to comply with its obligations to prevent, supress, and punish exploiters, because victims are not enabled to participate in prosecution processes against their exploiters. Further, when victims of trafficking are treated as criminals rather than as victims, they are placed outside of the protections available to victims which exist to prevent re-trafficking. In this way, by taking punitive actions towards victims of trafficking, the state actively creates an environment which is conducive to traffickers.

The sources of the definition of trafficking

The Palermo Protocol

The definition of trafficking can be traced to the "Palermo Protocol" to the UN Convention against Transnational Organised Crime. Both the Convention and the Palermo Protocol were adopted by the UN General Assembly on 15 November 2000.[1] The Palermo Protocol was the first global legally binding instrument with an agreed definition of trafficking.

---

1 Protocol to Prevent, Suppress and Punish Trafficking in Persons Especially Women and Children, supplementing the United Nations Convention against Transnational Organized Crime 2000.

The Palermo Protocol was signed by the United Kingdom on 14 December 2000, entered into force on 25 December 2003, and was ratified by the United Kingdom on 9 February 2006.[2] At Article 3 it provides definitions as follows:

> "(a) "Trafficking in persons" shall mean the recruitment, transportation, transfer, harbouring or receipt of persons, by means of the threat or use of force or other forms of coercion, of abduction, of fraud, of deception, of the abuse of power or of a position of vulnerability or of the giving or receiving of payments or benefits to achieve the consent of a person having control over another person, for the purpose of exploitation. Exploitation shall include, at a minimum, the exploitation of the prostitution of others or other forms of sexual exploitation, forced labour or services, slavery or practices similar to slavery, servitude or the removal of organs;
>
> (b) The consent of a victim of trafficking in persons to the intended exploitation set forth in subparagraph (a) of this article shall be irrelevant where any of the means set forth in subparagraph (a) have been used;
>
> (c) The recruitment, transportation, transfer, harbouring or receipt of a child for the purpose of exploitation shall be considered "trafficking in persons" even if this does not involve any of the means set forth in subparagraph (a) of this article;

2 United Nations, 'United Nations Treaty Collection' (*United Nations Treaty Collection*, 8 April 2022) <https://treaties.un.org/pages/ViewDetails.aspx?src=TREATY&mtdsg_no=XVIII-12-a&chapter=18&clang=_en> accessed 8 April 2022.

(d) "Child" shall mean any person under eighteen years of age."

This definition of trafficking in the Palermo Protocol can be broken down to give a definition which generally requires 3 components, as follows:

1. **The action of trafficking.** This can be recruitment, transportation, transfer, harbouring, or receipt of persons.

2. **The means of trafficking.** This can be the threat or use of force or other forms of coercion, of abduction, of fraud, of deception, of the abuse of power or of a position of vulnerability, or of the giving or receiving of payments or benefits to achieve the consent of a person having control over another person.

3. **This being for the purpose of exploitation.** This includes but is not limited to the prostitution of others or other forms of sexual exploitation, forced labour or services, slavery or practices similar to slavery, servitude, or the removal of organs.

As a result of the way that the Palermo Protocol is drafted, some nuances arise:

1. If the "means" are used, then the consent of a person to being trafficked is irrelevant to whether they were trafficked.

2. If the victim is a child, then the "means" are not required: "action" and "purpose of exploitation" are enough.

3. As a result of the combination of the above, if the victim is a child, the "means" are not used, and the victim consents to trafficking, they may not be treated as meeting the definition of trafficking.

Often overlooked in consideration of the Palermo Protocol is that its scope of application relates only to transnational offences of trafficking.[3] This is perhaps unsurprising, given the Palermo Protocol's origins in a convention aimed specifically at combatting transnational organised crime. However, the limited scope of the Palermo Protocol does not alter the definition of trafficking which it provides. Trafficking which is not transnational in nature still falls within the definition of trafficking contained within the Palermo Protocol. The limited scope of the Palermo Protocol merely means that it does not impose obligations on states to address trafficking exclusively within their own borders. The definition of trafficking that the Palermo Protocol contains is applied broadly in international and domestic law outside of transnational situations and cases involving organised criminal groups.

The European Convention against Trafficking

The Council of Europe's Convention on Action Against Trafficking in Human Beings[4] ("**ECAT**") aimed to improve the protection afforded by the Convention against Transnational Organized Crime and the Palermo Protocol, as well as to develop the standards established by them.[5] To achieve this aim, ECAT's scope is broader than the scope of the Palermo Protocol, applying to all forms of trafficking whether national or transnational, and whether or not connected with organised crime.[6] ECAT adopted in Article 4 the same definition of trafficking in human beings as the Palermo Protocol.

---

3 Palermo Protocol art 4.

4 Council of Europe Convention on Action against Trafficking in Human Beings 2005 (Council of Europe Treaty Series – No 197).

5 Council of Europe Convention on Action against Trafficking in Human Beings Preamble.

6 Council of Europe Convention on Action against Trafficking in Human Beings art 2.

ECAT came into force in February 2007, was ratified by the UK on 17 December 2008, and entered into force in respect of the United Kingdom on 1 April 2009.[7]

ECAT has not been incorporated into English domestic law and as a result cannot be relied upon directly in proceedings. However, it provides part of the interpretive guide to Article 4 of the ECHR, and is a basis for the definition of trafficking in the Modern Slavery Act 2015. As such, despite its lack of direct effect, its definition of trafficking and the rights set out in it guide how domestic law is to be interpreted. Moreover, insofar as the Secretary of State has adopted parts of ECAT as her own policy in guidance (see the section on The National Referral Mechanism below), the Secretary of State must follow that guidance unless there is good reason not to do so.[8]

The European Trafficking Directive

On 5 April 2011 the European Union adopted Directive 2011/36/EU on preventing and combating trafficking in human beings and protecting its victims ("**the Trafficking Directive**").[9] The Trafficking Directive recalled older International Labour Organization work on combatting forced labour, adopting a wider definition of trafficking in adults than the Palermo Protocol. In defining trafficking, it includes all of the actions, means, and purposes contained in the Palermo Protocol. It adds

---

7 Council of Europe, 'Chart of Signatures and Ratifications of Treaty 197' (*Treaty Office*, 7 February 2022) <https://www.coe.int/en/web/conventions/full-list> accessed 7 February 2022.

8 *R (G) v SSHD* [2016] 1 WLR 4031; (*R(O & H) v SSHD* [2019] EWHC 148 (Admin) [14].

9 Directive 2011/36/EU of the European Parliament and of the Council of 5 April 2011 on preventing and combating trafficking in human beings and protecting its victims, and replacing Council Framework Decision 2002/629/JHA 2011.

that the exchange or transfer of control over a person who has been subject to another action is included in the action of trafficking. It also specifies that exploitation includes the exploitation of criminal activities. The definition of trafficking it gives is as follows:

> "The recruitment, transportation, transfer, harbouring or reception of persons, including the exchange or transfer of control over those persons, by means of the threat or use of force or other forms of coercion, of abduction, of fraud, of deception, of the abuse of power or of a position of vulnerability or of the giving or receiving of payments or benefits to achieve the consent of a person having control over another person, for the purpose of exploitation.
>
> ...
>
> Exploitation shall include, as a minimum, the exploitation of the prostitution of others or other forms of sexual exploitation, forced labour or services, including begging, slavery or practices similar to slavery, servitude, or the exploitation of criminal activities, or the removal of organs."[10]

The Palermo Protocol definition includes but is not limited to specific types of exploitation and forced labour. Where the Trafficking Directive specifies additional types of exploitation as coming unambiguously within the definition of trafficking, this is complementary to the Palermo Protocol definition, rather than contradicting it.

---

10 Directive 2011/36/EU of the European Parliament and of the Council of 5 April 2011 on preventing and combating trafficking in human beings and protecting its victims, and replacing Council Framework Decision 2002/629/JHA art 2.

After the United Kingdom left the European Union, the Trafficking Directive was amended. Insofar as is relevant to the definition of trafficking, the amendment added the exploitation of surrogacy, of forced marriage, and of illegal adoption as explicit types of exploitation covered by the definition.[11] Again, this is complementary to the Palermo Protocol definition of trafficking, rather than contradicting it.

Although the United Kingdom initially exercised a right not to take part in the adoption of the Trafficking Directive and not to be bound by it,[12] the United Kingdom later decided to opt in to the Directive.[13] The Trafficking Directive came into force on 6 April 2013. After the United Kingdom left the European Union the "*rights, powers, liabilities, obligations, restrictions, remedies and procedures*" arising out of the Trafficking Directive continued in force by virtue of section 4 of the European Union (Withdrawal) Act 2018. In the leading cases on trafficking decided after the end of the implementation period (*R v Brecani*[14] and *R v AAD, AAH, and AAI*[15]), the continuing relevance of the Trafficking Directive for the interpretation of the United Kingdom's

11 Directive (EU) 2024/1712 of the European Parliament and of the Council of 13 June 2024 amending Directive 2011/36/EU on preventing and combating trafficking in human beings and protecting its victims 2024.

12 Directive 2011/36/EU of the European Parliament and of the Council of 5 April 2011 on preventing and combating trafficking in human beings and protecting its victims, and replacing Council Framework Decision 2002/629/JHA recital 35.

13 Commission Decision of 14 October 2011 on the request by the United Kingdom to accept Directive 2011/36/EU of the European Parliament and of the Council on preventing and combating trafficking in human beings and protecting its victims, and replacing Council Framework Decision 2002/629/JHA (notified under document C(2011) 7228).

14 *Brecani, R v* [2021] EWCA Crim 731, [2021] 1 WLR 5851.

15 *AAD, AAH, and AAI, R v* [2022] EWCA Crim 106, [2022] 1 WLR 4042.

international obligations in respect of the protection of victims of trafficking was not questioned by any party or by the court itself.

Subsequently, from 30 January 2023 to 31 December 2023 section 68(1) of the Nationality and Borders Act 2022 disapplied the "*rights, powers, liabilities, obligations, restrictions, remedies and procedures derived from the Trafficking Directive*" insofar as they were inconsistent with any provision made by or under the Nationality and Borders Act 2022. That provision has now been removed from domestic law through the Retained EU Law (Revocation and Reform) Act 2023 and secondary legislation made under it.

Nonetheless, the Trafficking Directive continues to be relevant to domestic law because it is used as an interpretive guide by the European Court of Human Rights ("**ECtHR**"), as set out below. The jurisprudence of the ECtHR remains binding on the United Kingdom.

The European Convention on Human Rights

Article 4 of the European Convention on Human Rights ("**ECHR**")[16] deals with the prohibition on slavery and forced labour. It provides insofar as is relevant:

> "1. No one shall be held in slavery or servitude.
>
> 2. No one shall be required to perform forced or compulsory labour."

Article 4 enshrines one of the "basic values of the democratic societies making up the Council of Europe" and gives rise to an absolute right.[17]

---

[16] Convention for the Protection of Human Rights and Fundamental Freedoms 1950.

[17] *Rantsev v Cyprus and Russia (no 25965/04)* (2010) 51 EHRR 1 [283].

The ECtHR uses a broad spectrum of international instruments as guides to the implementation of Article 4 of the ECHR in the context of trafficking. Chief among them is ECAT. The ECtHR has consistently treated ECAT as an interpretive guide to Article 4 ECHR in the context of trafficking, holding that "trafficking itself, within the meaning of Article 3(a) of the Palermo Protocol and Article 4(a) of the Anti-Trafficking Convention, falls within the scope of Article 4 of the Convention".[18] It has further held that the positive obligations derived from Article 4 ECHR must be considered within the broader context of ECAT and the Palermo Protocol.[19]

Subsequently, the ECtHR has used the Trafficking Directive as part of its interpretative framework for the rights derived from Article 4 ECHR.[20] Alongside these European materials which create strict obligations on states, the ECtHR takes account of a broad spectrum of international legal materials in its interpretation of the Article 4 ECHR rights in the trafficking context. These materials all reinforce the definition of trafficking given in the Palermo Protocol and ECAT.[21]

Domestic law: the Human Rights Act 1998

Sections 3 and 4 of the Human Rights Act 1998 place an obligation on domestic authorities, including courts, to interpret domestic law in accordance with ECHR rights and ECtHR case law. As such, the domestic interpretation of the definition of trafficking requires analysis of the method by which the ECtHR conducts its own interpretation. If

---

18 *Rantsev v Cyprus and Russia (no. 25965/04)* (n 17) para 282.

19 *Rantsev v Cyprus and Russia (no. 25965/04)* (n 17) para 285.

20 *VCL and AN v The United Kingdom (nos 77587/12 and 74603/12)* (2021) 73 EHRR 9; *GS v United Kingdom (no 7604/19)*; *SM v Croatia (no 60561/14)* (2021) 72 EHRR 1.

21 See e.g. *VCL and AN v The United Kingdom (nos. 77587/12 and 74603/12)* (n 20); *SM v Croatia (no. 60561/14)* (n 20).

domestic courts fail to take into account the ECtHR's interpretive approach, leading to them providing inconsistent interpretations which fail to protect victims of trafficking, then they may act unlawfully with regard to their obligations under the HRA 1998.

Domestic law: the Modern Slavery Act 2015

The Modern Slavery Act 2015 establishes a series of offences relating to slavery and trafficking, along with a defence to criminal conduct for certain trafficking victims. There are some material differences between the definitions provided by the text of the Modern Slavery Act 2015 and the Palermo Protocol and ECAT. We provide an explanation of these differences here because they can conceivably become relevant when the defence to criminal conduct for certain trafficking victims is being considered.

Section 1 provides for an offence of slavery, servitude and forced or compulsory labour, and section 2 for a separate offence of human trafficking.

The section 1 offence includes some sort of forced work.[22] Under section 1(2) references to slavery, servitude and forced and compulsory labour are to be construed in accordance with Article 4 of the ECHR. Under sections 1(3) and (4) regard shall be had to all the circumstances including any particular vulnerabilities which the victim has. Under section 1(5), "*The consent of a person (whether an adult or a child) to any of the acts alleged to constitute holding the person in slavery or servitude, or requiring the person to perform forced or compulsory labour, does not preclude a determination that the person is being held in slavery or servitude, or required to perform forced or compulsory labour.*"

The section 2 offence requires the arrangement or facilitation of the transportation of a person with a view to the victim being exploited.

---

[22] *Webb & Somerset-How, R v* [2025] EWCA Crim 1491 [79].

Therefore, for the section 2 offence, it is not necessary for any forced labour, or intended or foreseen exploitation, to actually take place. Under section 3, "exploitation" is defined as: slavery, servitude or forced or compulsory labour (s 3(2)); any sexual offence under Part 1 of the Sexual Offences Act 2003 or any offence of taking indecent photographs of children (s 3(3)); where the victim is required, encouraged or expected to give up any organ commercially (s 3(4)); or where the victim is "*subjected to force, threats or deception designed to induce him or her... to provide services of any kind...to provide another person with benefits of any kind, or...to enable another person to acquire benefits of any kind...having chosen him or her for that purpose on the grounds that...he or she is a child, is mentally or physically ill or disabled, or has a family relationship with a particular person, and...an adult, or a person without the illness, disability, or family relationship, would be likely to refuse to be used for that purpose*" (s 3(5) & (6)).

More so than the section 1 offence, under section 2(2) "*It is irrelevant whether V consents to the travel (whether V is an adult or a child)*".

As we explain below, the elements of the definition of human trafficking in the section 2 offence differ in limited respects from the elements of the definition of human trafficking in the international instruments. The section 2 offence creates offences in respect of most, but not all, conduct falling within the international definitions of trafficking. This may become relevant in certain very specific cases where a person wants to rely on the section 45 defence as a victim of human trafficking (rather than as a victim of slavery), but they cannot show that the particular conduct to which they were subject falls within the terms of section 2.

The discussion in the remainder of this section on the MSA 2015 is niche and technical, and can be skipped by readers who are not encountering the specific problem of whether a person satisfies the domestic definition of "victim of trafficking". We nonetheless include it for the sake of completeness.

Action

The actions proscribed by section 2 are the full range of actions set out in the Trafficking Directive ("*recruiting V, transporting, transferring, harbouring or receiving V, or transferring or exchanging control over V*"), rather than the more limited range set out in the Palermo Protocol and ECAT. However, those actions are only proscribed by section 2 insofar as the actions involve arranging or facilitating the "travel" of the victim. Pursuant to section 2(5), travel has a broad meaning, of (a) arriving in, or entering, any country, (b) departing from any country, or (c) travelling within any country. The Act does not provide a minimum distance which must be travelled.[23] Nonetheless, where no travel is arranged or facilitated, the action element of the definition of trafficking in section 2 is not satisfied. As such, under the MSA 2015, a person is not a victim of "human trafficking" if there is no travel arranged or facilitated. This is a clear difference with the situation in the Palermo Protocol, ECAT, and the Trafficking Directive.

It is not hard to imagine scenarios where trafficking may take place under the Palermo Protocol and ECAT definition but not under the MSA 2015 definition. People recruited online for online sexual exploitation in their own homes may not satisfy the "action" criterion of the MSA 2015, but would satisfy the action criterion in the Palermo Protocol and ECAT. The same may go for a "cuckooing" situation, where person who is in their own home is forced to allow its use for drug dealing.

In a limited number of cases this difference between the "action" requirement in international law and in the MSA 2015 may have consequences for people accused of engaging in criminal offences committed as a result of being trafficked. As we set out in Chapter 6 below, such people may ordinarily have a right to rely on the statutory defence in section 45 of the MSA 2015. The defence in section 45 of the MSA 2015 is available to those who offend as a result of being a victim

---

23 *Ali, R v* [2015] EWCA Crim 1279, [2015] 2 Cr. App. R. 33.

of slavery (which includes for this purpose servitude and forced or compulsory labour[24]) or a victim of human trafficking (i.e., a section 2 offence[25]). However, victims of trafficking under international law may not be entitled to rely on the statutory defence if the action of trafficking involved no travel, and may therefore be deprived of protection.

Some people who do not satisfy the definition of "victim of trafficking" in the MSA 2015 may nonetheless satisfy its definition of "victim of slavery" (which includes servitude and forced and compulsory labour). Whether a person is a victim of slavery is to be determined in line with Article 4 of the ECHR.[26] The caselaw of the ECtHR gives a broad definition to forced or compulsory labour, and so it is likely that if a person only failed to satisfy the definition of trafficking because there was no arranging or facilitating of their travel, they would likely still be able to be treated as a victim of forced or compulsory labour.

In *S.M. v. Croatia*[27] the ECtHR clarified that the notion of "forced or compulsory labour" aims to protect against instances of serious exploitation irrespective of whether they are related to the specific human-trafficking context.

In *Van der Mussele v Belgium* the ECtHR held that a starting point for interpreting Article 4 ECHR was that "all work or service which is exacted from any person under the menace of any penalty and for which the said person has not offered himself voluntarily" was forced or compulsory labour.[28]

---

24 Modern Slavery Act 2015 s 56(1).

25 Modern Slavery Act s 45(5) & 56(2).

26 Modern Slavery Act s 1(2).

27 *SM v Croatia (no. 60561/14)* (n 20).

28 *Van der Mussele v Belgium (no 8919/80)* (1984) 6 EHRR 163 [32].

In this light, most cases which do not fall within the definition of "victim of human trafficking" in the MSA 2015 are nonetheless likely to fall within the definition of "victim of slavery". However, it is conceivable that there will nonetheless be some cases which slip between these definitions. The victim of cuckooing who is recruited by means of abuse of power for the purpose of forced criminal exploitation may neither be a victim of trafficking nor of slavery under domestic law, despite being a victim of trafficking under international law.[29]

It must be recalled that the United Kingdom's international obligations apply to all victims of trafficking under international law, not just those who are victims of trafficking under the MSA 2015. As a result, even if a person slips between the cracks of the domestic law definitions of "victim of trafficking" and "victim of slavery", and so cannot access the defence for victims of trafficking set out in section 45 of the MSA 2015, they will still have all of the other rights to non-liability which we explain further in Chapters 2, 4, 5, and 6.

Means

Where certain types of exploitation are used, the MSA 2015 does not require means to be used for a person to fall within the definition of a victim of trafficking or slavery. The section 1 offence of slavery, servitude, or forced or compulsory labour does not require means. As for the section 2 offence, where the relevant exploitation constitutes certain sexual offences (section 3(3)), or certain offences relating to the removal of organs (section 3(4)), the means are also not required (section 3(3)).

Where a person is subject to force, threats, or deception, designed to induce them to provide services or benefits, or to enable another person to acquire benefits of any kind, the "means" of trafficking will be present (section 3(5)).

---

[29] See by analogy *Webb & Somerset-How, R v* (n 22).

Finally, where a person uses or attempts to use force, threats, or deception designed to induce the victim to provide services or benefits, or to enable another person to acquire benefits of any kind, the "means" of trafficking will be present. If a person has chosen their victim on the ground that the victim is a child, is mentally or physically ill or disabled, or has a family relationship with a particular person, and an adult, or a person without the illness, disability, or family relationship, would be likely to refuse to be used for that purpose, the means of trafficking will be present.[30]

These are the exclusive means relevant to the domestic definition of trafficking in the MSA 2015. Forms of coercion other than force, threats, or deception; abduction not involving force, threats, or deception; fraud not involving deception; and the abuse of power or of a position of vulnerability; and "the giving or receiving of payments or benefits to achieve the consent of a person having control over another person" are all means which exist in the Palermo Protocol and ECAT but not the MSA 2015.

As a result, again, there may be circumstances in which a person is a "victim of trafficking" in international law but not under the MSA 2015 because the definition of "means" in section 3 of the MSA 2015 is narrower than the international definition. As with the issue we set out above regarding the narrow definition of the "action" of trafficking in the MSA 2015, this may lead to people not being defined as a "victim of trafficking" under the MSA 2015, and therefore not having access to its protections under section 45, despite the United Kingdom having obligations of non-liability towards them under international law.

For the purpose of exploitation

Where means are required and exploitation is independent of the means, the types of exploitation that can satisfy section 3 of the MSA 2015 (relevant only to the section 2 offence and not the section 1 offence) are

30 Modern Slavery Act s 3(6).

limited in nature. As set out in sections 3(5) and (6), it appears that the exploitation is the provision of services or benefits, or enabling another person to acquire benefits of any kind. This is capable of interpretation consistent with the Palermo Protocol, ECAT, and the Trafficking Directive, but is not automatically so.

Domestic law: section 69 Nationality and Borders Act 2022

For a limited number of purposes in the Modern Slavery Act 2015 (in particular the identification of victims), pursuant to section 56(1) the definition of "victim of trafficking" is to be determined by reference to the Nationality and Borders Act 2022. In turn, section 69 NBA 2022 provides that "*victim of slavery*" and "*victim of human trafficking*" have the meanings given in regulations made by the Secretary of State. The Slavery and Human Trafficking (Definition of Victim) Regulations 2022 sets out these definitions:

> "2.— Victim of slavery
>
> (1) For the purposes of Part 5 of the 2022 Act, "*victim of slavery*" means a person who has been subjected to slavery, servitude or forced or compulsory labour.
>
> (2) In determining whether a person has been subjected to slavery, servitude or forced or compulsory labour, regard may be had to all the circumstances including—
>
> > (a) any of the person's personal circumstances (such as the person's age, the person's family relationships, and any physical or mental disability or illness) that significantly impair the person's ability to protect themselves from being subjected to slavery, servitude or forced or compulsory labour;
> >
> > (b) any work or services provided by the person.

(3) The consent of a person (whether an adult or a child) to any of the conduct alleged to show that the person has been subjected to slavery, servitude or forced or compulsory labour is not relevant to a determination as to whether the person is a victim of slavery.

3.— Victim of human trafficking

(1) For the purposes of Part 5 of the 2022 Act, "*victim of human trafficking*" means a person ("V") whose travel is arranged or facilitated by another person ("P")—

(a) using any of the methods mentioned in paragraph (5), and

(b) with a view to V being exploited.

(2) P may in particular arrange or facilitate V's travel by recruiting V, transporting or transferring V, harbouring or receiving V, or transferring or exchanging control over V.

(3) The consent of V (whether V is an adult or a child) to the travel is not relevant to a determination as to whether V is a victim of human trafficking.

(4) It is irrelevant for the purpose of paragraph (1)(a) whether the person using the method is P or another person.

(5) The methods are—

(a) in a case where V is an adult at the time the method is used—

(i) the threat or use of force or other coercive behaviour;

(ii) abduction, kidnap or false imprisonment;

(iii) fraud or other deception;

(iv) abuse of power or a position of vulnerability;

(v) the giving of payments or other benefits to achieve the consent of a person who has control over V;

(b) in a case where V is a child at the time the method is used, any method.

(6) For the purposes of paragraph (1)(b), a person is being exploited if the person is—

(a) prostituted by another person or otherwise subject to sexual exploitation;

(b) subjected to slavery or servitude or forced or compulsory labour;

(c) encouraged, required or expected to…do anything which involves the commission, by that person or another person, of an offence… of commercial dealings in organs and restrictions on use of live donors…

(d) subjected to force, threats or deception designed to induce that person—

(i) to provide services of any kind;

(ii) to provide another person with benefits of any kind, or

(iii) to enable another person to acquire benefits of any kind.

(7) For the purposes of paragraph (6)(a), a person is prostituted by another person ("A") where that person is compelled by A to offer or provide sexual services to a different person in return for payment or a promise of payment (whether to A or anyone else).

(8) For the purposes of paragraph (6)(a), a person is subject to sexual exploitation if... something is done to that person which involves the commission of an offence [of] ...indecent photographs of children... [and other sexual offences under part 1 of the Sexual Offences Act 2003 and analogous legislation in Scotland and Northern Ireland].

Again, these provisions require "travel", which is missing from any requirement within the international legal instruments.

Domestic law: Modern Slavery Statutory Guidance

Section 49(1) of the Modern Slavery Act 2015 requires the Secretary of State to issue guidance about indicators of trafficking, supporting victims of trafficking, and determining whether a person is a victim of trafficking.

The Modern Slavery Statutory Guidance, in version 4.3 at the time of us writing, now appears online at:

https://www.gov.uk/government/publications/modern-slavery-how-to-identify-and-support-victims/modern-slavery-statutory-guidance-for-england-and-wales-under-s49-of-the-modern-slavery-act-2015-and-non-statutory-guidance-for-scotland-and-northe.

The Statutory Guidance notes that "*Modern slavery encompasses human trafficking and slavery, servitude and forced or compulsory labour. Human trafficking consists of three basic components: action, means and purpose of exploitation. All three components must be present in an adult trafficking case; for child trafficking the 'means' component is not required*"

The Statutory Guidance goes on to provide that the definition of human trafficking, slavery, servitude and forced and compulsory labour is provided in The Slavery and Human Trafficking (Definition of Victim) Regulations 2022 and sets out the definition of human trafficking provided by Article 4 of ECAT.

CHAPTER TWO

OBLIGATIONS TOWARDS VICTIMS OF TRAFFICKING

The types of obligations towards victims of trafficking

Article 4 of the ECHR imposes three kinds of positive obligations on the State:[31]

- A general duty to implement measures to combat trafficking – "the systems duty";
- A duty to investigate situations of potential trafficking – "the investigation duty" (sometimes called "the procedural duty"); and
- A duty to take steps to protect individual victims of trafficking – "the protection duty" (sometimes called "the operational duty").

The systems duty

Article 4 of the ECHR generates a positive obligation on member states to effectively prosecute and penalise acts of trafficking.[32] In *Rantsev v Cyprus* it was held that:

> "In order to comply with this obligation, member States are required to put in place a legislative and administrative framework to prohibit and punish trafficking. The Court

---

31 *R (on the application of TDT) v Secretary of State for the Home Department* [2018] EWCA Civ 1395, [2018] 1 WLR 4922 [17].

32 *Siliadin v France (no 73316/01)* (2006) 43 EHRR 16 [112].

observes that the Palermo Protocol and the Anti-Trafficking Convention refer to the need for a comprehensive approach to combat trafficking which includes measures to prevent trafficking and to protect victims, in addition to measures to punish traffickers"[33]

Articles 5-7 and 9-12 of the Palermo Protocol provide for member states to implement various measures. These include the following:

- Criminalise acts of trafficking (Article 5);

- Provide victims of trafficking with information on relevant court and administrative proceedings and assistance to enable their views and concerns to be presented and considered at appropriate stages of criminal proceedings against offenders (Article 6.2);

- Provide for the physical, psychological and social recovery of victims of trafficking in persons, in particular appropriate housing, counselling about their legal entitlements, medical and psychological assistance, and employment, educational and training opportunities (Article 6.3);

- Offer victims of trafficking the possibility of obtaining compensation for damage suffered (Article 6.5);

- For state authorities, including law enforcement, to be trained in "methods used in preventing such trafficking, prosecuting the traffickers and protecting the rights of the victims, including protecting the victims from the traffickers" (Article 10.2).

ECAT provides for various measures throughout, including:

---

33 *Rantsev v Cyprus and Russia (no. 25965/04)* (n 17) para 285.

- To enable migration to take place legally (Article 5.4);
- To reduce children's vulnerability to trafficking, notably by creating a protective environment for them (Article 5.5);
- To discourage the demand that fosters all forms of exploitation of person (Article 6);
- To identify victims (Article 10);
- To assist victims in their physical, psychological and social recovery (Article 12);
- To allow victims a reflection and recovery period of at least 30 days when there are reasonable grounds to believe that the person concerned is a victim (Article 13);
- To give victims a right to legal assistance and to claim compensation from the perpetrators and/or from a central fund (Article 15);
- To criminalise acts of trafficking (Article 18), "use of services which are the object of exploitation….with the knowledge that the person is a victim of trafficking…" (Article 19), producing or procuring forged travel documents for use in trafficking (Article 20), or aiding and abetting any of those acts (Article 21);
- "Each Party shall, in accordance with the basic principles of its legal system, provide for the possibility of not imposing penalties on victims for their involvement in unlawful activities, to the extent that they have been compelled to do so" (Article 26);

- To protect victims and witnesses from potential retaliation or intimidation, including where appropriate by protecting their identity (Articles 28 and 30).

The investigation duty

Article 10 of ECAT deals with the investigation duty:

> "1 Each Party shall provide its competent authorities with persons who are trained and qualified in preventing and combating trafficking in human beings, in identifying and helping victims, including children, and shall ensure that the different authorities collaborate with each other as well as with relevant support organisations, so that victims can be identified in a procedure duly taking into account the special situation of women and child victims and, in appropriate cases, issued with residence permits under the conditions provided for in Article 14 of the present Convention.
>
> 2 Each Party shall adopt such legislative or other measures as may be necessary to identify victims as appropriate in collaboration with other Parties and relevant support organisations. Each Party shall ensure that, if the competent authorities have reasonable grounds to believe that a person has been victim of trafficking in human beings, that person shall not be removed from its territory until the identification process as victim of an offence provided for in Article 18 of this Convention has been completed by the competent authorities and shall likewise ensure that that person receives the assistance provided for in Article 12, paragraphs 1 and 2."

In *TV v Spain*,[34] in finding the state liable for breaching the procedural obligation, the ECtHR held that the procedural obligations with respect to victims of trafficking arise at the point that prima facie evidence of trafficking is brought the attention of the authorities, and not at the point that the investigation is completed:

> "92. In any event, the Court reiterates that a conclusion as to whether the domestic authorities' procedural obligation arose has to be based on the circumstances prevailing at the time when the relevant allegations were made or when the prima facie evidence of treatment contrary to Article 4 was brought to the authorities' attention and not on a subsequent conclusion reached upon the completion of the investigation or the relevant proceedings (see S.M. v. Croatia, cited above, § 325)…."

The protection duty and the evolution of the duty not to prosecute

As its name suggests, the UN Convention Against Transnational Organised Crime, to which the Palermo Protocol was attached, was aimed at promoting cooperation to prevent and combat transnational organised crime more effectively. Under Article 2(b), one of the purposes of the Protocol is to "*protect and assist the victims of such trafficking, with full respect for their human rights*". However, the Convention itself is concerned rather more with multinational cooperation in combatting organised crime and does not give much detail on the protection of victims. Victims feature substantively only in Article 25 of the Convention, which creates obligations on states to assist and protect victims against threats of retaliation or intimidation, to allow for compensation and restitution, and to allow for the views of victims to be presented in proceedings. These protections for victims seem to be aimed

34 *TV v Spain (no 22512/21)* [2025] Crim LR 96.

at the Convention's primary purpose of combatting organised crime. In the preparation of the Convention they elicited little discussion.[35]

Although the Palermo Protocol provides the fundamental globally agreed definition of trafficking, it did little to set out specific enforceable rights for victims of trafficking who are forced into criminality. Indeed, its definition of exploitation did not explicitly include forced criminal exploitation. This must be seen in light of its role as a Protocol to a convention on organised crime rather than a document created specifically to deal with the protection of victims of trafficking.

Nevertheless, the inclusion in its stated purpose of Article 2(b) to "*protect and assist the victims of such trafficking, with full respect for their human rights*" was significant. In 2009 the Working Group on Trafficking in Persons, which was set up to advise and assist the Conference of the Parties to the Convention in the implementation of its mandate with regard to the Palermo Protocol, recommended:

> "12. With regard to ensuring the non-punishment and nonprosecution of trafficked persons, States parties should:
> (a) Establish appropriate procedures for identifying victims of trafficking in persons and for giving such victims support;
> (b) Consider, in line with their domestic legislation, not punishing or prosecuting trafficked persons for unlawful acts committed by them as a direct consequence of their situation as trafficked persons or where they were compelled to commit such unlawful acts [...]."[36]

---

[35] United Nations Office on Drugs and Crime, 'Travaux Préparatoires of the Negotiations for the Elaboration of the United Nations Convention against Transnational Organized Crime and the Protocols Thereto' (United Nations 2006) 251.

[36] Working Group on Trafficking in Persons, 'Report on the Meeting of the Working Group on Trafficking in Persons Held in Vienna on 14 and 15

In 2010 the Working Group reaffirmed what it had said in 2009, and went further stating:

> "51. States parties should ensure that, provisions for the non-punishment and non- prosecution of trafficked persons contained in domestic legislation, guidelines, regulations, preambles or other instruments were clearly stated. In doing so, States parties are encouraged to make use of technical assistance tools such as the UNODC Model Law against Trafficking in Persons and principles and guidelines such as the Recommended Principles and Guidelines on Human Rights and Human Trafficking of the Office of the United Nations High Commissioner for Human Rights, as well as any other regional standards and guidelines."[37]

Much further detail as to specific protections to be given to victims of trafficking was set out in ECAT. Article 12 of ECAT provides for assistance to be given to victims including subsistence and psychological assistance. Article 13 provides for a "*recovery and reflection period of at least 30 days, when there are reasonable grounds to believe that the person concerned is a victim.*" Most significantly for the purposes of this book, Article 26 requires states to provide for the possibility of not imposing penalties on victims of trafficking for criminal offences they have been compelled to commit, as follows:

April 2009' (Conference of the Parties to the United Nations Convention against Transnational Organized Crime 2009) CTOC/COP/WG.4/2009/2.

[37] Working Group on Trafficking in Persons, 'Report on the Meeting of the Working Group on Trafficking in Persons Held in Vienna from 27 to 29 January 2010' (Conference of the Parties to the United Nations Convention against Transnational Organized Crime 2010) CTOC/COP/WG.4/2010/6.

> "Article 26 – Non-punishment provision
>
> Each Party shall, in accordance with the basic principles of its legal system, provide for the possibility of not imposing penalties on victims for their involvement in unlawful activities, to the extent that they have been compelled to do so."

In *Rantsev v Cyprus and Russia*[38] the ECtHR held that Article 4 of the ECHR places positive obligations on states to protect against human trafficking, including by requiring "*a State to take operational measures to protect victims, or potential victims, of trafficking*" where the state was "*aware, or ought to have been aware, of circumstances giving rise to a credible suspicion that an identified individual had been, or was at real and immediate risk of being, trafficked or exploited*".

The Trafficking Directive provides at recital 14 (emphasis added):

> "Victims of trafficking in human beings should, in accordance with the basic principles of the legal systems of the relevant Member States, **be protected from prosecution or punishment for criminal activities** such as the use of false documents, or offences under legislation on prostitution or immigration, **that they have been compelled to commit as a direct consequence of being subject to trafficking.** The aim of such protection is to safeguard the human rights of victims, to avoid further victimisation and to encourage them to act as witnesses in criminal proceedings against the perpetrators. This safeguard should not exclude prosecution or punishment for offences that a person has voluntarily committed or participated in."

[38] *Rantsev v Cyprus and Russia (no. 25965/04)* (n 17) para 286.

Article 8 of the Trafficking Directive creates an obligation on states to ensure that prosecutors and courts are entitled not to prosecute or impose penalties on victims of trafficking. This is wider than a mere non-punishment obligation. It provides:

> "Non-prosecution or non-application of penalties to the victim
>
> Member States shall, in accordance with the basic principles of their legal systems, take the necessary measures to ensure that competent national authorities are entitled not to prosecute or impose penalties on victims of trafficking in human beings for their involvement in criminal activities which they have been compelled to commit as a direct consequence of being subjected to any of the acts referred to in Article 2."

In 2013, the Office of the Special Representative and Co-ordinator for Combating Trafficking in Human Beings at the Organization for Security and Co-operation in Europe noted that:

> "It is often a deliberate strategy of the traffickers to expose victims to the risk of criminalization and to manipulate and exploit them for criminal activities. It is therefore not uncommon that victims of trafficking commit criminal offences or other violations of the law directly connected with, or arising out of, their trafficking situation. In these situations they often come to the attention of the authorities primarily as offenders and they may not be easily recognized as actual victims of a serious crime... The non-punishment of victims of trafficking for offences they have committed as a consequence, or in the course, of being trafficked is an essential element of...a human rights approach.
>
> ...

> The punishment of victims of trafficking for crimes directly related to their trafficking is a violation of their fundamental dignity. It constitutes a serious denial of reality and of justice. Such punishment blames victims for the crimes of their traffickers, for crimes that, but for their status as trafficked persons, they would not have perpetrated. The criminalization of trafficked victims may be tantamount to persecution of victims by the State: not only does it fail to take into account the serious crimes committed against the victim by the traffickers, which should be investigated, it fails to recognize trafficked persons as victims and witnesses of those serious crimes and exacerbates their victimization and/or trauma by imposing on such persons State-imposed, unjust punishment. Instead of being treated as victims, they are treated as criminals. This practice furthermore promotes trafficking in human beings by failing to confront the real offenders, by dissuading trafficked victims from giving evidence against their traffickers and by enabling traffickers to exert even further control over their victims by threatening exposure to punishment by the State."[39]

In *VCL and AN v The United Kingdom*,[40] the ECtHR held that, through Article 4 ECHR, states' international obligations to consider non-liability became justiciable rights to non-liability held by victims of trafficking. In particular, the ECtHR held that states' positive obligations under Article

---

39 Office of the Special Representative and Co-ordinator for Combating Trafficking in Human Beings, 'Policy and Legislative Recommendations towards the Effective Implementation of the Non-Punishment Provision with Regard to Victims of Trafficking' (Organization for Security and Co-operation in Europe (OSCE) 2013).

40 *VCL and AN v The United Kingdom (nos. 77587/12 and 74603/12)* (n 20).

4 of the ECHR must be construed in light of ECAT.[41] The ECtHR went on to hold that prosecution itself may violate Article 4 of the ECHR:

> "159....the prosecution of victims, or potential victims, of trafficking may, in certain circumstances, be at odds with the state's duty to take operational measures to protect them where they are aware, or ought to be aware, of circumstances giving rise to a credible suspicion that an individual has been trafficked."
>
> "162. Once a trafficking assessment has been made by a qualified person, any subsequent prosecutorial decision would have to take that assessment into account. While the prosecutor might not be bound by the findings made in the course of such a trafficking assessment, the prosecutor would need to have clear reasons which are consistent with the definition of trafficking contained in the Palermo Protocol and the Anti-Trafficking Convention for disagreeing with it."[42]

One effect of the decision in *VCL and AN v the UK* in domestic law is that a violation of the non-liability protection is itself unlawful, by virtue of section 6 of the Human Rights Act 1998. This is so from the point when prima facie evidence of treatment contrary to Article 4 is first brought to the authorities' attention. In *TV v Spain*,[43] in finding liability for breaching the procedural obligation, the Court provided the following guidance (emphasis added):

41 *VCL and AN v The United Kingdom (nos. 77587/12 and 74603/12)* (n 20) para 150.

42 *VCL and AN v The United Kingdom (nos. 77587/12 and 74603/12)* (n 20) paras 159–162.

43 *TV v Spain (no. 22512/21)* (n 34).

> "92. In any event, the Court reiterates that a conclusion as to whether the domestic authorities' procedural obligation arose has to be based on the circumstances prevailing at the time when the relevant allegations were made or when the prima facie evidence of treatment contrary to Article 4 was brought to the authorities' attention and not on a subsequent conclusion reached upon the completion of the investigation or the relevant proceedings (see S.M. v. Croatia, cited above, § 325)...."

As such, the procedural obligation will be breached when the State ought to have been aware of the circumstances giving rise to a credible suspicion of trafficking.

CHAPTER THREE

THE IMPLEMENTATION OF THE INVESTIGATIVE DUTY THROUGH THE NATIONAL REFERRAL MECHANISM

The National Referral Mechanism

On 1 April 2009, with the coming into force of ECAT, the UK Government created the National Referral Mechanism ("**NRM**") and associated guidance. The NRM is a process whereby evidence submitted about potential victims of trafficking is assessed by a Competent Authority in order to decide whether the person is to be recognised as a victim of trafficking. At that time, the only Competent Authority was the Single Competent Authority. Subsequently, in November 2021, the Immigration Enforcement Competent Authority was created to deal with some Foreign National referrals.

Since 2022 the guidance in force has been various versions of "*Modern Slavery: Statutory Guidance for England and Wales (under s49 of the Modern Slavery Act 2015) and Non-Statutory Guidance for Scotland and Northern Ireland "Victims of Modern Slavery – Competent Authority Guidance*"[44] ("the Modern Slavery Statutory Guidance"). That guidance

[44] 'Modern Slavery: Statutory Guidance for England and Wales (under S49 of the Modern Slavery Act 2015) and Non-Statutory Guidance for Scotland and Northern Ireland (Accessible Version)' (*GOV.UK*, 24 December 2025) <https://www.gov.uk/government/publications/modern-slavery-how-to-identify-and-support-victims/modern-slavery-statutory-guidance-for-england-and-wales-under-s49-of-the-modern-slavery-act-

consistently refers to ECAT. The guidance replaced a previous guidance document "*Victims of modern slavery – Competent Authority guidance*" which had explicitly made clear that it was based on ECAT.[45]

Making a referral

Only a specified "First Responder" can make a referral to the NRM. A full list of first responders is given in the "National referral mechanism guidance: adult (England and Wales)"[46] and includes the police, the Home Office, local authorities, and a small handful of charities, but not solicitors.

If a defendant or suspect has not been referred to the NRM despite indicators of trafficking then the prosecution will sometimes say that the defence solicitors need to make the referral. This is wrong. Defence solicitors are not able to make a referral. The best they can do is write to the Salvation Army or another of the listed charities to ask them to make the referral. The waiting time just for a referral in this way tends to be several months.

In any event, the investigative duty is held by arms of the state, including the police, from the point that they are made aware of evidence giving rise to a credible suspicion of trafficking. If the prosecution or police have been made aware of indicators and have failed to make a referral, particularly before making the decision to charge, then they are in breach

---

2015-and-non-statutory-guidance-for-scotland-and-northe> accessed 29 December 2025.

45 Home Office, 'Victims of Modern Slavery: Competent Authority Guidance, Version 8.0'.

46 'National Referral Mechanism Guidance: Adult (England and Wales)' (*GOV.UK*) <https://www.gov.uk/government/publications/human-trafficking-victims-referral-and-assessment-forms/guidance-on-the-national-referral-mechanism-for-potential-adult-victims-of-modern-slavery-england-and-wales> accessed 11 December 2025.

of the investigative duty and should be reminded of this. A claim for damages under Article 4 ECHR should also be explored.

Once a referral has been made, solicitors should send the competent authority any relevant evidence including:

- Representations setting out the defendant's account in detail, in particular highlighting the connection between the trafficking and the alleged offence; and

- Evidence of vulnerability to trafficking such as: Education, Health, and Care Plans (**EHCPs**); relevant medical records; or expert psychological or psychiatric assessments obtained for criminal proceedings.

This is to assist the competent authority in making a positive decision which is sufficiently detailed, and which covers the alleged offending. It is incredibly frustrating to wait months or even years for a conclusive grounds decision only for it to come back in a form which does not assist, because it does not cover the things it needs to. The best way to avoid this is to provide all relevant material at the outset of the referral process.

The decision-making process

The Modern Slavery Statutory Guidance outlines the NRM decision-making process for the Single Competent Authority and the Immigration Enforcement Competent Authority as follows.

Following a referral from a First Responder Organisation, the competent authority will decide whether there are reasonable grounds to suspect that a person is a victim of trafficking. The test is lower than the balance of probabilities. The decision should be made within 5 days, where possible.[47]

After a positive reasonable grounds decision, there follows a Recovery Period of at least 30 calendar days during which in theory the potential victim will be entitled to support.[48] In practice the support is limited to not being removed from the country. Many potential victims are remanded in custody during the 30 days' Recovery Period with no support at all.

There follows a decision as to whether there are conclusive grounds to believe that the person is a victim of trafficking. This decision is made on the balance of probabilities. If there is not enough evidence in the initial referral form to make the decision then the Modern Slavery Statutory Guidance provides that the competent authority "*must make every reasonable effort to request all available information that could prove useful in establishing if there are Conclusive Grounds*", including by asking the potential victim or their legal representative for further information[49] In many cases the competent authority will delay for a long time before making further enquiries with the police, immigration authorities, or the potential victim. A previous version of the Statutory Guidance explicitly provided that the process of enquiry should begin during the 30-day recovery period. Although the current version does not include that provision, where the competent authority has unreasonably delayed

47 'Modern Slavery: Statutory Guidance for England and Wales (under S49 of the Modern Slavery Act 2015) and Non-Statutory Guidance for Scotland and Northern Ireland (Accessible Version)' (n 44) para 7.4 & 7.6.

48 'Modern Slavery: Statutory Guidance for England and Wales (under S49 of the Modern Slavery Act 2015) and Non-Statutory Guidance for Scotland and Northern Ireland (Accessible Version)' (n 44) para 7.8.

49 'Modern Slavery: Statutory Guidance for England and Wales (under S49 of the Modern Slavery Act 2015) and Non-Statutory Guidance for Scotland and Northern Ireland (Accessible Version)' (n 44) para 14.138. See also 14.137 & 14.58.3.

making further enquiries, particularly while the potential victim is in custody pending the decision, there may be scope for a claim for breach of Article 4 of the ECHR, for false imprisonment, or for a judicial review of the delay.

As to the ending of support for recovery, in theory, "*following a positive Conclusive Grounds decision, victims will be exited from support only when appropriate to do so. Victims with a positive Conclusive Grounds decision will receive at least 45 calendar days of support during the move-on support period.*"[50]

Delay

A problem very often facing defendants to criminal proceedings is a lengthy delay in obtaining a conclusive grounds decision. Older versions of the Modern Slavery Statutory Guidance provided a target of 45 days for a conclusive grounds decision to be made. However more recent versions of the guidance provide that there is "no target" but that "*When the relevant competent authority has received sufficient information for it to complete a decision it should seek to do so as soon as possible but only once a minimum of 30-calendar days of the Recovery Period have passed*".[51]

Where an individual is on bail, a conclusive grounds decision will typically take over a year, and often several years. In September 2025 (the latest data available at the time of writing), the average age of a case

---

[50] 'Modern Slavery: Statutory Guidance for England and Wales (under S49 of the Modern Slavery Act 2015) and Non-Statutory Guidance for Scotland and Northern Ireland (Accessible Version)' (n 44) para 7.1.

[51] 'Modern Slavery: Statutory Guidance for England and Wales (under S49 of the Modern Slavery Act 2015) and Non-Statutory Guidance for Scotland and Northern Ireland (Accessible Version)' (n 44) para 14.124.

awaiting a conclusive grounds decision was 141 days.[52] That was down by more than half compared to the previous quarter.[53]

The delay in obtaining a conclusive grounds decision can have very significant consequences, particularly in the context of criminal proceedings. Where a defendant is on bail awaiting trial, bail conditions can be onerous. For children, even without onerous bail conditions, the delay can be disastrous. Criminal bail for a drugs or weapons offence can often mean exclusion from education, and for an older child, delay could mean they turn 18, at which point they will be dealt with by adult services.

Where an individual is in custody, the competent authority operates a priority list which means that the decision should be made before the custody time limit or the trial.[54] Practically speaking, this usually means a wait of over 5 months on remand in custody. This disproportionately affects people without immigration status, because it is they who are usually deemed a "flight risk" and so the threshold test is applied for charging.

---

52 'Modern Slavery: National Referral Mechanism and Duty to Notify Statistics UK, Quarter 3 2025 – July to September' (*GOV.UK*, 6 November 2025) <https://www.gov.uk/government/statistics/modern-slavery-nrm-and-dtn-statistics-july-to-september-2025/modern-slavery-national-referral-mechanism-and-duty-to-notify-statistics-uk-quarter-3-2025-july-to-september> accessed 11 December 2025.

53 'Modern Slavery: National Referral Mechanism and Duty to Notify Statistics UK, Quarter 2 2025 – April to June' (*GOV.UK*, 2 September 2025) 2 <https://www.gov.uk/government/statistics/modern-slavery-nrm-and-dtn-statistics-april-to-june-2025/modern-slavery-national-referral-mechanism-and-duty-to-notify-statistics-uk-quarter-2-2025-april-to-june> accessed 11 December 2025.

54 *R (on the application of FH) v Secretary of State for the Home Department* [2024] EWHC 1327 (Admin) [6, 87, 147, 154–158].

Recent challenges to very lengthy delays in conclusive grounds decisions have been refused. However, no challenge to delay involving an applicant facing criminal charges has yet reached the courts. Helpful comments which could be relied on in such a challenge in future were made in *R (on the application of O and H) v SSHD*:[55]

> "108. In my judgment the fact that there are some additional advantages that may flow from a positive Conclusive Grounds decision does not make the delay in the system unlawful. There is no evidence that potential victims of trafficking are, in fact, liable to prosecution after the grant of a Reasonable Grounds decision. There are advantages in the grant of discretionary leave to remain, but those advantages are less obvious when the comparator status is being a person in respect of whom a Reasonable Grounds decision has been made."

By contrast, where a potential victim of trafficking is the defendant to criminal proceedings arising out of that trafficking, there is a clear benefit to being granted a positive conclusive grounds decision as compared with a positive reasonable grounds decision. That is because the prosecution guidance instructs that "*Once a person has been identified as a potential victim, a decision on whether to prosecute them should, so far as possible, be taken after the relevant competent authority's decision has been taken.*"[56] Moreover in such cases the delay will often cause a very clear detriment, most obviously where the defendant is on remand in custody, but also for example where they are subject to restrictive bail conditions or

55 *R (on the application of O and H) v Secretary of State for the Home Department* [2019] EWHC 148 (Admin).

56 Crown Prosecution Service, 'Modern Slavery and Human Trafficking: Offences and Defences, Including the Section 45 Defence' (22 July 2025) <https://www.cps.gov.uk/prosecution-guidance/modern-slavery-and-human-trafficking-offences-and-defences-including-section> accessed 11 December 2025.

excluded from education. In such cases, particularly where there has been a failure to take reasonable steps to gather evidence, a challenge to the delay may have merit.

Public Order Disqualification

Article 13 of ECAT provides for a recovery and reflection period of at least 30 days after an assessment that there are reasonable grounds to believe an individual may be a victim of trafficking. However, the state is "*not bound to observe this period if grounds of public order prevent it or if it is found that victim status is being claimed improperly.*"[57]

Section 63 of the Nationality and Borders Act 2022 (**NABA 2022**) provided for the first time for a person who has received a positive reasonable grounds decision to be disqualified from the reflection and recovery period on grounds of public order. Section 63(3) provides that "*the circumstances in which a person is a threat to public order include, in particular*", where a person has been convicted in the United Kingdom of any offence listed in Schedule 4 of the Modern Slavery Act 2015, or a corresponding offence elsewhere; or where a person is a foreign criminal within the meaning given by section 32(1) of the UK Borders Act 2007, which means that they have received a sentence of at least 12 months' immediate custody for any offence. That will include, for example, almost anyone convicted of arriving in the UK without entry clearance before later being trafficked, for which the starting point at sentence is a period of 12 months' immediate custody.[58] It will also include those who the state failed to recognise as a potential victim of trafficking and therefore prosecuted without making an NRM referral. Due to the fact that anyone who has ever been convicted of a Schedule 4 offence will also be included, no matter the circumstances of the conviction, even a victim of trafficking who many years before as a child committed a non-violent

---

[57] Council of Europe Convention on Action against Trafficking in Human Beings art 13(3).

[58] *Ginar (Aydin), R v* [2023] EWCA Crim 1121, [2024] 1 WLR 1264.

robbery which resulted in a referral order would be potentially excluded from protection.

Under section 63(2) of NABA, the effect of a public order disqualification is that the person can then be removed from the United Kingdom. The previous version of the Modern Slavery Statutory Guidance provided that it would also remove the obligation to make a conclusive grounds decision.[59] The result of this was catastrophic for criminal appeals, which will most often depend on a conclusive grounds decision which post-dates conviction. However in *R (on the application of ABW) v Secretary of State for the Home Department* it was held that the secretary of state remains under an obligation to proceed to a conclusive grounds decision in respect of a potential victim of trafficking for so long as that person remained in the UK, even after a public order disqualification decision has been made.[60] Following ABW, on 23 December 2025 decision-making on public order disqualifications was paused until further notice.[61]

---

59 'Modern Slavery: Statutory Guidance for England and Wales (under S49 of the Modern Slavery Act 2015) and Non-Statutory Guidance for Scotland and Northern Ireland (Accessible Version)' (n 44) para 14.242.

60 *R (on the application of ABW) v Secretary of State for the Home Department* [2025] EWHC 3280 (Admin).

61 'Modern Slavery: Statutory Guidance for England and Wales (under S49 of the Modern Slavery Act 2015) and Non-Statutory Guidance for Scotland and Northern Ireland (Accessible Version)' (n 44), top of page.

PART TWO

THE PROSECUTION JOURNEY

CHAPTER FOUR

THE PRE-CHARGE STAGE

Speed is essential in defending victims of forced criminal exploitation. Where a person is arrested on suspicion of a criminal offence, and there are indicators of trafficking, it is essential that a referral is made into the NRM as soon as possible. A referral should be made whenever there are indicators of trafficking. It should be made before the decision to charge.

What happens next depends on which test is applied for charging. There are two tests applied by the Crown Prosecution Service when deciding whether to charge a person with a criminal offence; the "Full Code Test" and the "Threshold Test". The Full Code Test is applied when the relevant information is available to the prosecutor to make a charging decision. The Threshold Test is applied when the seriousness or circumstances of the case justify the making of an immediate charging decision, and there are substantial grounds to object to bail. If the Threshold Test has been applied, then the Full Code Test must subsequently be applied as soon as any anticipated further evidence or material is received, and in any event in Crown Court cases before the service of the prosecution case.

The Full Code Test

The decision to charge is governed by the guidance document "*Director's Guidance on Charging*".[62] This sets out the charging process at section 4 and the "Full Code Test" for charging most cases at section 5. A decent

---

62 'Director's Guidance on Charging' (December 2020) <https://www.cps.gov.uk/prosecution-guidance/directors-guidance-charging-sixth-edition-december-2020-incorporating-national> accessed 11 December 2025.

rule of thumb is that, if the case is a bail case, the Full Code Test will apply.

The *Director's Guidance on Charging* provides at section 7 and Annex 6 that prosecutors may advise the police about potential charges (7.1) and that advice given before the charging decision is "*early advice*" (7.2). It states that the provision of early advice is "*strongly recommended*" in '*Modern Slavery and Human Trafficking including cases involving exploitation where charges under the Modern Slavery Act 2015 are under consideration e.g. in the context of "county lines" supply of controlled drugs*" but also that these cases "*must be referred to the relevant CPS Area or Casework Division for a charging decision. It is imperative that the relevant CPS Area or Casework Division is contacted to discuss referral arrangements for all these case types, particularly if an immediate charging decision is needed and early advice was not obtained.*"[63]

The Threshold Test

For cases where a charging decision needs to be made more quickly, usually where there are serious objections to bail pending charge, the *Directors Guidance on Charging* provides for the "Threshold Test" to be used.[64] This applies "*to a very limited range of cases where the Full Code Test cannot be met but the overall seriousness or circumstances of the case justify the making of an immediate charging decision, and there are substantial grounds to object to bail.*"[65] Five conditions must be met:

63 'Director's Guidance on Charging' (n 62) Annex 6 para 1.

64 'Director's Guidance on Charging' (n 62) s 6.

65 'Director's Guidance on Charging' (n 62) s 6.1.

1. There are reasonable grounds to suspect that the person to be charged has committed the offence, including consideration of any defence which has been put forward;[66]

2. Further evidence can be obtained to provide a realistic prospect of conviction;[67]

3. The seriousness of the circumstances of the case justified the making of an immediate charging decision;[68]

4. There are continuing substantial grounds to object to bail in accordance with the Bail Act 1976 and in all the circumstances of the case it is proper to do so;[69] and

5. It is in the public interest to charge the suspect. "*Prosecutors must apply the public interest stage of the Full Code Test based on the information available at that time.*"[70]

It follows that where the Threshold Test is applied, there is no need to wait for a conclusive grounds decision.

---

[66] 'Director's Guidance on Charging' (n 62) s 6.6.

[67] 'Director's Guidance on Charging' (n 62) s 6.7.

[68] 'Director's Guidance on Charging' (n 62) s 6.8.

[69] 'Director's Guidance on Charging' (n 62) s 6.9.

[70] 'Director's Guidance on Charging' (n 62) s 6.10.

The application of the Crown Prosecution Service's guidance on modern slavery and human trafficking

The Crown Prosecution Service has produced a guidance document on prosecuting victims of trafficking, "*Modern Slavery and Human Trafficking: Offences and Defences*".[71] It notes that:

> "Once a person has been identified as a potential victim, a decision on whether to prosecute them should, so far as possible, be taken after the relevant competent authority's decision has been taken. This is particularly important where the suspect is a child. The European Court of Human Rights (ECtHR) held in VCL and AN v United Kingdom (2021) 73 E.H.R.R. 9 that "... in the absence of any assessment of whether they were trafficked and, if so, whether that fact could have any impact on their criminal liability, ... pleas [made before such as assessment] were not made "in full awareness of the facts".
>
> However, each case must be considered in accordance with the Code for Crown Prosecutors on its own facts. If a competent authority's decision on a suspected victim is pending, paragraph 4.3 of the Code should be considered: the charging decision should only follow all outstanding reasonable lines of inquiry being pursued, unless the prosecutor is satisfied that any further evidence or material is unlikely to affect the application of the Full Code Test, whether in favour of or against a prosecution.
>
> In the limited circumstances where it is appropriate to apply the Threshold Test, there should be a rigorous examination of all five conditions in paragraph 5 of the Code. Scrutiny of

[71] Crown Prosecution Service, 'Modern Slavery and Human Trafficking: Offences and Defences, Including the Section 45 Defence' (n 56).

> each of the conditions is critical to ensuring that cases are not charged prematurely. The decision to apply the Threshold Test must remain under review and the Full Code Test must be applied as soon as the anticipated further material is received."

There is an obvious internal contradiction between the requirement of the first paragraph of the guidance quoted above, which is based on binding caselaw, and the guidance that follows. Whereas the first paragraph requires delay pending the outcome of a conclusive grounds decision with limited exceptions, the subsequent paragraphs permit reliance on the Threshold Test without a prior determination of whether, if a person was to be found to be a victim of trafficking, prosecution would be appropriate. This can lead to premature charging decisions and the remand in custody of victims of trafficking. As such, this guidance appears to run counter to the intention of the ECtHR as set out so clearly in the first quoted paragraph above.

Despite this internally contradictory approach in the Crown Prosecution Service guidance, the clear legal position is that when a conclusive grounds decision is pending, the decision to charge should so far as possible be delayed. A failure to wait for a conclusive grounds decision would be liable to amount to a violation of a victim of trafficking's rights to non-prosecution.

Remanding a person in custody is coercive. Where any eventual sentence would be short, pleading guilty may result in less time in prison than pleading not guilty and being acquitted after trial. As such, remand pending trial can coerce a guilty plea, violating the right to non-punishment. It is arguable that remand alone, followed by the discontinuation of proceedings or acquittal, could amount to a violation of the right to non-punishment because the practical effect on a victim of trafficking in terms of loss of liberty would be the same as in the event of conviction.

In practice, people likely to be remanded, especially non-British citizens trafficked to the United Kingdom – will be charged despite an outstanding NRM referral. These individuals suffer the greatest harm from this policy, as they may spend 5–6 months in prison awaiting a conclusive grounds decision.

Representations should therefore be made not to apply the Threshold Test. Where there are clear indicators of trafficking, particularly if a suspect has put forward an account of being exploited, conditions (1) and (5) of the Threshold Test may not be satisfied. Destitute foreign nationals are often deemed a flight risk due to lack of accommodation, but if the suspect has claimed asylum, they may qualify for housing under sections 95 or 98 of the Immigration and Asylum Act 1999 or Schedule 10 of the Immigration Act 2016. In such cases, measures could mitigate absconding risk, meaning condition (4) may also not be met.

Considerations in the police interview

There are many reasons not to give an account in a police interview. Although it can lead to an adverse inference being drawn that the defendant had no good explanation, juries are directed not to draw that inference if there is another reasonable explanation and not to convict solely on the basis of an adverse inference. Late disclosure is particularly common for victims of trafficking who may still be under the influence of their traffickers.

However, in modern slavery or human trafficking cases, a police interview or a prepared statement setting out the bare bones of the exploitation can be extremely helpful. When representations to discontinue are made, the Crown Prosecution Service will often say that there is no evidence of modern slavery or human trafficking (even where there are clear indicators) and refer to the no comment interview. Even on appeal in trafficking cases, a failure to give disclosure in police interview has been held against an appellant when deciding whether his account of being trafficked was true.[72]

In a magistrates' or youth court case where there has been a no comment interview, but instructions have been given relating to trafficking, practitioners should prepare a voluntary defence statement at the earliest opportunity to mitigate the prejudice caused by the lack of comment at interview stage.

72 *BNN, R v* [2024] EWCA Crim 991 [68, 76].

CHAPTER FIVE

RUNNING ABUSE OF PROCESS POST-CHARGE AND UP TO TRIAL

The wait for a decision

Victims of trafficking face long waits to be recognised as such by the criminal legal system (see section on delay in Chapter 3). A mere assertion by a suspect that they are a victim of trafficking will not stop a prosecution against them. Nor will the existence of obvious indicators of trafficking, or a positive reasonable grounds decision. In practice, the Crown Prosecution Service will generally not begin to reconsider prosecuting a victim of trafficking until they are in possession of a positive conclusive grounds decision. This fact, taken with the typically long delays for conclusive grounds decisions, means that victims of forced criminal exploitation face years awaiting trial. The lucky ones may spend that time on bail, often subject to onerous bail conditions. This can be particularly damaging to children who may face exclusion from school and be placed at risk of re-trafficking if they are not removed from the situation of exploitation. The unlucky ones will spend many months remanded to prison, suffering additional persecution by the state consequent on the state's failure to protect them from trafficking.

In cases where there are clear indicators of trafficking, but the prosecutor is refusing to exercise their discretion to discontinue proceedings before receiving a conclusive grounds decision, practitioners should consider bringing claims for breach of Article 4 of the ECHR. If criminal defence practitioners feel unable to do so themselves, then they should refer clients to experts in the field. Meanwhile, there are important practical steps that should be taken while waiting for a conclusive grounds decision.

Representations to the competent authority

For a victim facing prosecution as a result of forced criminal exploitation, it can be devastating to wait months or even years for a positive conclusive grounds decision only to realise that the decision fails to comment on the part of their exploitation relevant to their defence. Even though lawyers cannot refer an individual into the NRM (see "Making a referral" in Chapter 3 above), that does not leave lawyers powerless to ensure that the conclusive grounds decision will be relevant to the criminal proceedings. With authorisation from their client, lawyers can write to the competent authority to provide further evidence. Representations which set out a defendant's account in detail can be extremely helpful in obtaining an accurate and focussed conclusive grounds decision that considers the nexus between the trafficking and the criminal allegations against the victim of trafficking.

Preparing expert reports

Expert reports can and should be sent to the competent authority to assist them in making their decision. The most helpful reports are commonly psychiatric reports, psychological reports, and reports from modern slavery and human trafficking experts. Criminal defence solicitors can secure legal aid funding for such reports in circumstances when the reports will be used in representations to discontinue proceedings or at trial. See Chapter 6 for more information on the use that can be made of expert reports at trial.

Reports from psychiatrists and psychologists

Psychiatric and psychological reports are relevant to the consideration of the trafficking claim by the competent authority because people with some mental health conditions or neurodivergence are more likely to be vulnerable to trafficking. Many victims of trafficking will have post-traumatic stress disorder as a result of their experiences, in which case a report may also corroborate their account. Substance abuse issues are also relevant, as debt bondage resulting from addiction is common.

It is often helpful to have reports from both a forensic psychiatrist (who is able to diagnose mental health conditions) and a psychologist (who is able to comment on neurodivergence, suggestibility, maturity in relation to chronological age, and adjustments needed for trial). Some clinical psychologists will be able to do both.

Experts should be asked to interview the defendant, to separately interview any parental figure or significant other, and to review medical, educational, and social care records. Psychiatrists should be asked to provide a full diagnosis, comment on causation and the possibility of malingering, and, where relevant, to comment on fitness to plead. Psychologists should be asked to comment on any neurodivergence or cognitive impairments, and to comment on suggestibility and maturity in relation to chronological age. It is often helpful to ask experts whether the individual is likely to be more suggestible or vulnerable to exploitation than another person of their age and sex as a result of any mental health, neurodivergence or cognitive issue: this would generally be admissible evidence at trial. Psychologists' reports tend to be more detailed than psychiatrists' reports. It can be helpful to obtain the psychiatrist's report first, and then provide it to the psychologist, so that the psychologist can also comment on the relevance of the mental health diagnosis.

Reports from modern slavery and human trafficking experts

Experts in modern slavery and human trafficking should be asked to explain how the type of trafficking to which the defendant was subjected works in practice. In so far as is relevant to the case, they should comment on the type of person who is likely to be vulnerable to that type of trafficking, and provide an overview of indicators of trafficking. They should not express a view on whether or not the defendant is telling the truth about having been trafficked.

Vacating trial dates

Where a date for trial approaches, but a conclusive grounds decision has not yet been made, the trial will need to be vacated. This tends to be agreed. If a detailed application is needed, reliance can be placed on the caselaw outlined under "The systems duty" in Chapter 2 above, as well as the Crown Prosecution Service's Guidance discussed in the section on "Delay" in Chapter 3 above.[73] Note that the Single Competent Authority operates a prioritisation system whereby decisions will generally be made by the trial date, so before an application to vacate is made, efforts should be made to ensure that the competent authority is aware of the trial date and to ask them for a timescale.[74] The application should not be made prematurely.

Defence statements and requests for disclosure

The Crown Prosecution Service often relies on a lack of "*evidence*" in support of the defence case when refusing to discontinue, citing a no comment interview, despite the fact that victims of trafficking are known often to provide late disclosure. In our experience, this has been the case even where there are very strong indicators of trafficking. A defence statement can provide the necessary evidential basis, and in the magistrates' court or youth court, voluntary defence statements should generally be provided.

The defence statement should raise abuse of process as a possible legal issue and set out that disclosure of the prosecutor's reasons for continuing (if they do continue) should be disclosed. Other relevant disclosure to request from the prosecutor may include previous convictions of co-defendants or the alleged trafficker, any other allegations against co-

[73] Crown Prosecution Service, 'Modern Slavery and Human Trafficking: Offences and Defences, Including the Section 45 Defence' (n 56).

[74] *R (on the application of FH) v Secretary of State for the Home Department* (n 54) paras 6, 87, 147, 154–158.

defendants or the alleged trafficker, and the steps taken to investigate the defendant's trafficking claim. An absence of investigation by the police into the defendant's trafficking may constitute a violation of the Article 4 ECHR right, but may also provide part of the basis for an abuse of process argument, or a defence at trial.

Representations to discontinue

Generally speaking, representations to the Crown Prosecution Service should be made after a positive conclusive grounds decision so that it can be taken into account. In some cases with strong indicators of trafficking, particularly where the defendant is in custody or the wait on bail for trial is having a very detrimental impact on them, it may be worth making representations before the conclusive grounds decision is received. The prosecutor will almost certainly say that they will not make a decision until after the conclusive grounds decision as their guidance instructs them to do so.[75] However, in so doing they are arguably acting in breach of Article 4 of the ECHR, particularly where the potential victim is held in custody. This is because the procedural duties under Article 4 of the ECHR arise at the point when the prima facie evidence of trafficking is brought to the authorities' attention, not at the point when the investigation is concluded.[76]

Representations to the prosecution should highlight the relevant part of the conclusive grounds decision and the expert reports and walk the prosecution through their guidance "*Modern Slavery and human trafficking: offences and defences*".[77] This is supposed to integrate the non-

---

75 Crown Prosecution Service, 'Modern Slavery and Human Trafficking: Offences and Defences, Including the Section 45 Defence' (n 56).

76 *TV v Spain (no. 22512/21)* (n 34) para 92.

77 Crown Prosecution Service, 'Modern Slavery and Human Trafficking: Offences and Defences, Including the Section 45 Defence' (n 56).

punishment duty into the law of England and Wales. It sets out a four-stage test for decisions to prosecute in the following terms:

> "1. Is there a reason to believe that the person is a victim of modern slavery?
>
> If yes, move to Question 2.
>
> If not, you do not need to consider this assessment further.
>
> 2. Is there clear evidence of a credible common law defence of duress?
>
> If yes, then the case should not be charged or should be discontinued on evidential grounds.
>
> If not, move to Question 3.
>
> 3. Is there clear evidence of a statutory defence under section 45 of the 2015 Act?
>
> If yes, then the case should not be charged or should be discontinued on evidential grounds
>
> If not, move to Question 4.
>
> 4. Is it in the public interest to prosecute? This must be considered even where there is no clear evidence of duress, or all the elements of the statutory defence under section 45, or where the offence is excluded under Schedule 4."

The previous version of the guidance used to direct prosecutors at stage 4 to "consider all the circumstances of the case, including the seriousness of the offence and any direct or indirect compulsion arising from their trafficking situation".[78] We suggest that the removal of this provision from the Guidance should not change how it should be applied, as a failure to consider all the circumstances of the case would likely be a public law error.

Representations will often focus on the public interest stage of the test, particularly where an offence is excluded from the section 45 defence under Schedule 4 of the Modern Slavery Act 2015. The guidance provides as follows:

> "Prosecutors should apply the factors in the Code for Crown Prosecutors with specific consideration of the following:
>
> - the seriousness of the offence
> - the level of culpability of the suspect
> - the harm caused to the victim
> - the suspect's age and maturity
>
> Additionally, prosecutors should consider the following...
>
> - Whether there is a nexus or connection between the trafficking/slavery or past trafficking/slavery and the alleged offending; and, if so,
> - Whether the force of compulsion from the trafficking/slavery or past trafficking/slavery acting

[78] Crown Prosecution Service, 'Modern Slavery, Human Trafficking and Smuggling' (*The National Archives*, 22 January 2022) <https://webarchive.nationalarchives.gov.uk/ukgwa/20220122231648/https:/www.cps.gov.uk/legal-guidance/modern-slavery-human-trafficking-and-smuggling> accessed 30 December 2025.

> on the suspect is enough to remove their culpability/criminality or reduce their culpability/criminality to a point where it is not in the public interest to prosecute them. …

'Compulsion' includes all the means of trafficking defined by the Palermo Protocol. It does not require physical force or constraint.

The means of trafficking/slavery (i.e. the level of compulsion) may not be sufficient to give rise to defences of duress or under section 45 but will be relevant when considering the public interest test.

A suspect's criminality or culpability should be considered in light of the seriousness of the offence. The more serious the offence, the greater the compulsion needed to reduce the criminality or culpability to the point where it is not in the public interest to prosecute.

When assessing the public interest in respect of a child victim, it is not necessary for there to have been compulsion… Accordingly, if Stage 4 is reached for a child, prosecutors should consider:

- whether there is a nexus or connection between the trafficking/slavery or past trafficking/slavery and the alleged offending; and, if so,

- whether the circumstances remove the child's culpability/criminality or reduce it to a point where it is not in the public interest to prosecute them. If there was compulsion, then this will reduce the public interest, but it is not a necessary element. As for an adult, the more serious the offence, the

> stronger the mitigating factors will need to be before it is not in the public interest to prosecute."[79]

This guidance provides significant difficulties in cases involving children, and the guidance itself or its application in particular cases may be susceptible to challenge. As set out in Chapter 1, in the case of children the definition of "trafficking" which the United Kingdom is required to apply by the international legal sources does not require the "means" of trafficking to be present. As such, the focus on compulsion that still exists in the guidance in respect of children is wholly misplaced. In cases involving children, once the trafficking nexus is established, the focus must be on protection and the best interests of the child.

Applications to stay proceedings

Where there is a positive conclusive grounds decision but the prosecutor will not discontinue proceedings, an application may be made to the court to stay proceedings as an abuse of process. The court, as a public authority, is required not to act unlawfully, and therefore to take steps to regulate its own procedure in order to prevent unlawful actions which would result in the violation of ECHR rights (in this case, Article 4).

In *R v AAD, AAH, and AAI*[80] the Court of Appeal confirmed that the abuse of process jurisdiction was available where a decision to prosecute a victim of trafficking had been taken, in particular where a conclusive grounds decision was available or had subsequently been made. It provided guidance as follows:

> "141. As a matter of procedure, on an application to stay the proceedings, for instance on the basis that the Crown had unjustifiably failed to take into account the CPS Guidance

---

[79] Crown Prosecution Service, 'Modern Slavery and Human Trafficking: Offences and Defences, Including the Section 45 Defence' (n 56).

[80] *AAD, AAH, and AAI, R v* (n 15).

when deciding to prosecute, one option available to the judge prior to making a decision would be to adjourn the application to afford the CPS the opportunity to reconsider/remake its decision in light of its own guidance. This approach may be less appropriate, however, if the contention is that the decision was simply unsustainable or perverse.

142. We draw the threads together. Our conclusions on this ground are as follows:

(1) The limb two abuse of process jurisdiction remains available in principle in all VOT cases following the 2015 Act, and whether or not they are Schedule 4 cases.

(2) Such jurisdiction is "special" only in the sense that it falls to be exercised in the context of a particular sensitivity required to be applied to VOT prosecutions, having regard to international obligations and specific CPS guidance. The core requirements of unfairness and oppression and illegality (inherent in almost every limb two case) remain central to applications for a stay in a VOT context.

(3) Mere disagreement with a decision to prosecute, following due regard given by the prosecution to the CPS guidance and to any conclusive grounds decision, gives no basis whatsoever for an application for a stay. Decisions to prosecute are for the CPS. Decisions on disputed facts or evaluations of fact are for the jury.

(4) If (in what will be likely to be a most exceptional case) there has been a failure to have due regard to CPS guidance or if there has been a lack of rational basis for departure by the prosecution from a conclusive grounds decision then a stay application may be available. It will then be assessed by

> the court, by way of review on grounds corresponding to public law grounds."

This was summarised in R v AFU[81] as:

> "the decision to prosecute is ultimately for the prosecution, and not the court. Where the prosecution has applied its mind to the relevant questions in accordance with the applicable CPS guidance, it will not generally be an abuse of process to prosecute unless the decision to do so is "clearly flawed"... However, if CPS guidance has been disregarded, such that the question of whether to prosecute has not been properly considered (or considered at all), the court can intervene more readily: see AGM at [13] and [56]. It will then be open to the court to consider the public interest question without trespassing on ground which has been appropriately considered by the prosecution authorities."[82]

> "It is not, however, 'for the appellate court to substitute its own view, but rather to review the decision to prosecute by reference to considerations of including those of rationality and procedural fairness'"[83]

One practical issue we have on occasion (although not recently) faced is persuading the prosecutor to give written reasons for continuing a prosecution which can then be challenged. If this issue arises then the case of VCL and AN v UK[84] at paragraph 162 is helpful.

---

81 *AFU, R v* [2023] EWCA Crim 23.

82 *AFU, R v* (n 81) para 113.

83 *AFU, R v* (n 81) 117.

84 *VCL and AN v The United Kingdom (nos. 77587/12 and 74603/12)* (n 20).

Once the defence have access to the reasons for a decision to continue a prosecution, they will need to scrutinise them. It may be a case where, rather than making an application to stay, a further NRM referral is needed because the original referral was not detailed enough or did not cover the alleged offending. This will depend on the reasons that the prosecutor has given for continuing. Alternatively, the prosecutor may disagree that the individual is a victim of trafficking, stating that the evidence upon which the conclusive grounds decision is based is insufficient or incomplete. It may be possible to challenge this in an abuse of process application or judicial review on the basis that it is arbitrary – because one arm of the state is disagreeing with another – or on its merits. Alternatively, it may be better to re-refer the matter to the competent authority to ask them to update their decision based on further evidence.

The prosecutor may agree that the individual is a victim of trafficking but find that there is no nexus between the trafficking and the offence. If that is because of a lack of detail in the conclusive grounds decision then further representations should be made to the competent authority and they should be asked to reconsider their decision. Relevant considerations would include the length of time between the trafficking and the offence, and how the trafficking gave rise to the offence.

The prosecutor may agree that the individual is a victim of trafficking and find that there is a nexus between the trafficking and the offence, but conclude that it is still in the public interest to prosecute. This will usually be because the "force of compulsion" is not enough to "reduce their culpability to a point where it is not in the public interest to prosecute them". When confronting this argument in a subsequent application to stay proceedings, it may be helpful to note that the compulsion can include, "threat or use of force or other coercion", as stated in the Palermo Protocol. It explicitly does not need to amount to the level of threat necessary for a defence of duress to be made out, and it can include debt bondage. Bear in mind also that, where the defendant is a child, that will be the wrong test entirely: this seems obvious, but we have encountered cases where this has happened.

Judicial review of refusal to stay proceedings

Matters relating to trial on indictment in the Crown Court cannot be judicially reviewed, but matters relating to summary trial in youth courts and the magistrates' courts can be. Where an application to stay proceedings has been refused by a youth court or magistrates' court, a judicial review of the refusal to stay can be brought.

The authorities distinguish between two types of interlocutory judicial review. Decisions about how magistrates hear a case (e.g. admissibility of evidence) are not amenable to interlocutory judicial review. Decisions about whether magistrates should hear and determine a case are amenable to judicial review.[85]

It will be necessary to weigh up whether judicial review is necessary, in the sense that waiting for the trial to conclude and then, if necessary, appealing the case in the Crown Court by way of rehearing (see Chapter 8) would not be an adequate alternative remedy. It will often be the case that an appeal after conviction would not be an adequate alternative remedy because it would require the person to first be convicted and serve any sentence, contrary to the non-punishment principle in Article 4 of the ECHR. Moreover, Article 4 of the ECHR entails a non-prosecution duty, and so in certain circumstances a trial, even one which results in a not guilty verdict, could breach Article 4 of the ECHR. The following factors, or a combination of them, would further strengthen an argument that there is no adequate alternative remedy to a judicial review:

---

85 *R (on the application of Hoar-Stevens) v Richmond upon Thames Magistrates' Court* [2003] EWHC 2660 (Admin) [16].

- The defendant is a child, as contact with the criminal legal system is particularly detrimental for children.[86]

- The defendant is particularly vulnerable and will find the trial process particularly difficult.

- The defendant faces exclusion from education as a result of pending proceedings or conviction.

- A custodial sentence is likely.

- The defendant is of good character.

The pleadings in judicial reviews against a court which refuses to stay proceedings and against the prosecutor would be broadly the same. However, there are important tactical considerations about which of the court or the prosecutor should be the defendant to the judicial review.

A judicial review against the prosecutor should seek relief in the form of a mandatory order for the reconsideration of the decision to prosecute. If the prosecutor was ordered to reconsider the decision to prosecute (or if they offered to do so without being ordered) then they could remake the same decision, but in a manner which was more difficult to challenge. For example, if the prosecutor had originally decided to prosecute because they irrationally concluded that a person was not a victim of trafficking, a new decision-maker could accept that the person was a victim of trafficking and that there was a nexus between the trafficking and the offending but could find that it was nonetheless in the public interest to prosecute. In such circumstances, the judicial review would

[86] See, e.g. Committee on the Rights of the Child, 'General Comment No. 24 (2019) on Children's Rights in the Child Justice System' (United Nations 2019) CRC/C/GC/24 para 2; Sentencing Children and Young People Guideline para 1.4, 1.6, 1.8.

have been successful but would bring no benefit to the person on whose behalf it was brought.

In contrast, a judicial review against the trial court, with the Crown Prosecution Service as an interested party, will ask for relief in the form of a mandatory order for the trial court to stay proceedings. In such a judicial review the trial court is almost certain not to alter its decision to refuse a stay by providing better reasoning, and such an action may in any event be perceived as improper *ex post facto* rationalisation. Further, the prosecutor may be less likely to reconsider their decision to prosecute with a view to making it lawful, as it will not be the focus of the judicial review. Any reconsideration of the prosecutor's decision to prosecute would be less relevant to the judicial review, which should focus on the court's decision. As a result, in such circumstances a successful judicial review may stand a chance of causing a stay of proceedings.

Therefore, in most circumstances, the remedy for a victim of trafficking will be more effective in a judicial review against a court's unlawful decision not to stay proceedings than in a judicial review against the prosecutor's decision to prosecute.

CHAPTER SIX

THE TRIAL PROCESS

Introduction

This chapter is intended only as a brief summary of defences available at trial. It is included in order to allow appeal lawyers to reference how the case should have been run. Appeal lawyers should be checking whether adequate advice was given on the section 45 and other defences, and on applications to stay.

We take the opportunity to remind practitioners that the point of the defences is not a "get out of jail free card". As we have set out above, the non-liability obligations are one part of the suite of obligations that the United Kingdom has towards victims of trafficking. If non-liability obligations are ignored, then victims are deprived of their other rights as victims of trafficking, such as to reflection and recovery, and a state of affairs is allowed to exist where traffickers operate with impunity. Defences at trial exist not just to prevent the criminalisation of individual victims of trafficking, but to create an environment in which trafficking is disincentivised. As such, where the United Kingdom has failed in its non-liability obligations towards an individual victim, it may indicate broader failings in relation to preventing trafficking more generally.

Expert evidence

See Chapter 5 for guidance on which experts should be instructed and what topics they should be asked to consider. As regards admissibility at trial, the basic principles are (1) that the report must be compliant with Part 19 of the Criminal Procedural Rules and Practice Direction 19, and (2) that the evidence must go to matters outside the knowledge of the jury.

Expert evidence which is on the face of it inadmissible, or admissible, is summarised in the table below:

Inadmissible	Admissible
According to *R v AAD, AAH, AAI*:[87] • "plausibility and consistency of the defendant's account" • "the vulnerability of the defendant" • "whether a given set of facts meets the legal definition of trafficking"	According to *R v Brecani*:[88] • "context of a cultural nature" • "societal and contextual factors outside the ordinary experience of the jury" According to *R v AAD, AAH, AAI*:[89] • "the defendant's psychiatric or psychological state" • "the detailed mores of people trafficking gangs operating in countries that are outside the court's own knowledge and experience"

Defences

For both the section 45 defence and duress, the evidential burden is on the defence but the legal burden is on the prosecution. This means that it is for the defendant to raise evidence of each of the elements of the

[87] *AAD, AAH, and AAI, R v* (n 15) para 86.

[88] *Brecani, R v* (n 14) para 58.

[89] *AAD, AAH, and AAI, R v* (n 15) para 87.

defence, and for the prosecution to disprove one or more of the elements to the criminal standard.[90]

Section 45 of the Modern Slavery Act 2015

Section 45 (1) provides that an **adult** (a person aged 18 or over at the time of the alleged offence) is not guilty of an offence if they do the act because they are compelled to do it, the compulsion is attributable to slavery or to relevant exploitation, and a reasonable person in the same situation as the person and having the person's age, sex and any physical or mental illness or disability would have no realistic alternative to doing that act.

Under section 45(2), a person may be compelled to act by another person or by the person's circumstances. An example of compulsion by circumstances is in *R v BYA*[91] wherein it was held that the appellant had been compelled to act as a result of her circumstances where she used a false identity document to attempt to flee from her traffickers.

Section 45(4) provides that a **child** (a person aged under 18 at the time of the alleged offence) is not guilty of an offence if they did the offence as a direct consequence of being, or having been, a victim of slavery or a victim of relevant exploitation, and a reasonable person in the same situation as the child and having the child's age, sex, and any physical or mental illness or disability would do that act. For a child, there is no requirement to show any degree of compulsion, and any focus on compulsion would amount to a fundamental error of legal analysis.

Under section 45(3), compulsion is attributable to slavery or to relevant exploitation only if (a) it is part of conduct which constitutes an offence of slavery, servitude or forced or compulsory labour under section 1 of the Modern Slavery Act 2015 or conduct which would constitute

---

[90] *MK, Gega, R v* [2018] EWCA Crim 667, [2019] QB 86 [45].

[91] *BYA, R v* [2022] EWCA Crim 1326.

"relevant exploitation", meaning exploitation attributable to being a victim of human trafficking or (b) it is a direct consequence of a person being, or having been, a victim of slavery or relevant exploitation.

Schedule 4 of the Modern Slavery Act 2015 provides that the defence under section 45 will not apply to specific listed offences, including most problematically:

- Robbery, burglary, violent disorder, and section 4 of the Public Order Act 1986 (putting people in fear of violence), and firearms offences, all of which commonly affect young people who are exploited under county lines.

- Assisting unlawful entry to the UK, although the boys who pilot small boats are often trafficked, and manslaughter, which is charged when those boats are wrecked.[92]

As the Modern Slavery Act 2015 came into force on 31 July 2015, the defence under section 45 is not available for offences committed before that date.[93]

Of course, it must be remembered that section 45 of the Modern Slavery Act 2015 does not limit the United Kingdom's obligations towards victims of trafficking. Even if a person falls outside the terms of the section 45 defence, or they are excluded from its protections because they are charged with an offence listed in Schedule 4, international law continues to require protection from prosecution and punishment wherever the necessary nexus with trafficking is established. Exclusion from the statutory defence does not diminish the importance of the non-

---

92 Kevin Rawlinson, 'Prosecutors Target Smuggled People Who Were Forced to Pilot Small Boats' (*The Guardian*, 23 February 2024) <https://www.theguardian.com/world/2024/feb/23/people-smuggling-gangs-small-boats-home-office-migration> accessed 11 December 2025.

93 *CS, Le, R v* [2021] EWCA Crim 134.

punishment principle. As such, even if the section 45 defence is not available, the other ways of mounting a defence, including by way of an application to stay, may be pursued.

Duress

The elements are as follows:

- **The defendant apprehends a threat of death or very serious injury** to them or a member of their immediate family or someone for whom they might reasonably feel responsible.[94] The threat can be from another person or from the defendant's circumstances.[95]

- **In the circumstances as the defendant believes them to be, there is no reasonable evasive action that the defendant could take,** like running away or calling the police.[96] The Crown Court Compendium states that "*It should be made clear to juries that if the retribution threatened against the defendant or their family, or a person for whom D feels responsible, is not such as D reasonably expects to follow immediately or almost immediately on their failure to comply with the threat, there may be little if any room for doubt that D could have taken evasive action, whether by going to the police or in some other way, to avoid committing the crime with which D is charged*".[97] However, immediately does not require immediacy in time; rather it is to do with whether there is any other reasonable option. In *R v Abdul-Hussain* it was held that while it is a requirement that imminent peril of death be operating on the

[94] *Brandford, R v* [2016] EWCA Crim 1794, [2017] 4 WLR 17.

[95] *Martin, R v* (1989) 88 Cr App R 343.

[96] *Johnson (Jennifer Nancy), R v* [2022] EWCA Crim 832.

[97] 'Crown Court Compendium Part I – October 2025' paras 18–3.4(2).

Defendant's mind at the time he commits the act, the risk does not need to be immediate:

> "...if Anne Frank had stolen a car to escape from Amsterdam and has been charged with theft, the tenets of English law would not have denied her a defence of duress of circumstances, on the ground that she should have waited for the Gestapo's knock on the door."[98]

- **The threat is the direct cause of the offence**, although it does not need to be the only cause.[99]

- **A sober person of reasonable firmness of the defendant's age, sex and character would have been driven to act as the defendant did.** As for relevant characteristics, the law has reached an inconsistent place where some mental health conditions will be included, and some will not. In *R v Bowen*[100] it was held that post traumatic stress disorder (common in trafficking cases) would be relevant to this assessment. Further, in *R v Antar*[101] it was held that suggestibility should be relevant where it is put not merely "*on the basis of [the defendant's] very low IQ, but on the basis of the psychologist's opinion that he functioned cognitively at a significantly impaired level; that he had a moderate (now a mild) learning disability; and importantly, that he had a level of suggestibility sufficiently higher than that of the general population*". Practitioners should have these issues in mind when drafting instructions for medical experts.

---

[98] *Abdul-Hussain (Mustafa Shakir), R v* [1998] EWCA Crim 3528 12.

[99] *Ortiz, R v* (1986) 83 Cr App R 173.

[100] *Bowen, R v* [1997] 1 WLR 372 379.

[101] *Antar, R v* [2004] EWCA Crim 2708 [46].

Offence-specific statutory defences

Section 31 of the Immigration and Asylum Act 1999 provides a defence to some immigration offences. It was intended to integrate the provision under Article 31 of the Refugee Convention[102] not to prosecute or punish asylum seekers who have fled directly to a safe country and have claimed asylum without delay. The defence will be made out where (i) the defendant is a genuine refugee; (ii) the defendant could not reasonably have claimed asylum in any country through which they passed *en route* to the UK (a short stopover will not cause the defence to fail); and (iii) the defendant presented themselves to the UK authorities without delay.

Under section 31(7) of the 1999 Act, where an asylum claim is pending or has been allowed, the burden of proof for the issue of whether the defendant is or is not a refugee lies on the defence, but the legal burden lies on the prosecution, to the criminal standard.[103] The Crown Prosecution Service's guidance "Immigration" provides that:[104]

> "If the defendant claims to be a refugee and no determination has been made, the Crown's position should be that while not accepting the claim or making any concessions in respect of their refugee status, the Crown will not seek to establish that they are not a refugee for the purpose of the criminal trial. In such cases there will be no issue for the jury to decide and no need to explain the term: R v Makuwa [2006] EWCA Crim 175 [37]."

---

102 Convention Relating to the Status of Refugees 1951.

103 *Makuwa, R v* [2006] EWCA Crim 175, [2006] 1 WLR 2755 [26]; *Mateta, R v* [2013] EWCA Crim 1372, [2014] 1 WLR 1516 [9, 21(i)].

104 Crown Prosecution Service, 'Immigration' (13 February 2024) <https://www.cps.gov.uk/prosecution-guidance/immigration> accessed 12 December 2025.

However, where an asylum claim has been refused, the legal burden lies on the defence to the balance of probabilities to prove the defendant is a refugee.[105] Therefore, where an asylum claim has been refused but an appeal is pending, the trial should be vacated.

The Nationality and Borders Act 2022 disapplied this defence to some very common offences, notably the offence of arriving without entry clearance. However, in all cases, the Crown must apply their guidance which sets out, in a similar way to the guidance on trafficking, when it will and will not be in the public interest to prosecute, and purportedly integrates the requirement under Article 31 of the Refugee Convention. The burden and standard of proof as to whether the Defendant is a refugee are the same as would apply to a section 31 defence at trial. Representations, applications to stay, and judicial review will be available to the defence practitioner in a similar way to that set out in Chapter 5 above, but based on the "Immigration" guidance.[106]

Directions

The Crown Court Compendium provides example directions and route to verdict which should be provided to the jury. For a section 45 defence it provides an example route to verdict as follows: [107]

> "Question 1: Has the prosecution made you sure that D was not a victim of human trafficking/modern slavery?
>
> - If the answer is yes, then your verdict will be guilty.

---

[105] *Sadighpour, R v* [2012] EWCA Crim 2669, [2013] 1 WLR 2725 [38–40]; *Mateta, R v* (n 103) paras 10, 21(i).

[106] Crown Prosecution Service, 'Immigration' (n 104).

[107] 'Crown Court Compendium Part I – October 2025' (n 97) 18–34 to 18–35.

- If the answer is no, go on to consider question 2.

Question 2: Has the prosecution made you sure that D was not compelled to cultivate the cannabis by reason of being a victim of human trafficking/modern slavery?

- If the answer to the question is yes, then your verdict will be guilty.

- If the answer to the question is no, go on to consider question 3.

Question 3: Has the prosecution made you sure that a reasonable person of D's age and sex and in the same situation as D {and having D's physical or mental illness or disability – outline any relevant evidence} would have had a realistic alternative to assisting in the cultivation of cannabis?

- If the answer to the question is yes, then your verdict will be guilty.

- If the answer to the question is no, then your verdict will be not guilty."

In cases where there is no dispute that the defendant is a victim of modern slavery, question 1 can be dispensed with.

Example directions and route to verdict for duress are at pages 18-20 – 18-21. Where there is no dispute that the defendant is a victim of modern slavery, separate directions for duress may not be required.

No example directions or route to verdict are provided for the section 31 defence. The following route to verdict may be appropriate:

"Question 1: Has the prosecution made you sure that D was not a genuine refugee?

- If the answer is yes, then your verdict will be guilty.
- If the answer is no, go on to consider question 2.

Question 2: Has the prosecution made you sure that D could not reasonably have claimed asylum in any country through which they passed en route to the UK?

- If the answer to the question is yes, then your verdict will be guilty.
- If the answer to the question is no, go on to consider question 3.

Question 3: Has the prosecution made you sure that D did not present themselves to the UK authorities without delay?

- If the answer to the question is yes, then your verdict will be guilty.
- If the answer to the question is no, then your verdict will be not guilty."

Defence practitioners should ensure that the court is directed to the relevant routes to verdict, and should scrutinise the route to verdict before the jury are sent into retirement. In considering an appeal, the accuracy of the route to verdict will almost always be a relevant consideration.

PART THREE

APPEALS

CHAPTER SEVEN

IDENTIFYING CASES FOR APPEAL

How cases can come to light

Although some trafficking appeals come to the attention of defence practitioners because they are referred to us as trafficking appeal cases, more commonly cases arise in other contexts, and the existence of an appeal related to trafficking status only becomes apparent on closer inspection.

A case may come to you directly for an appeal for other reasons. When assessing a case for the possibility of an appeal, it is always worth bearing in mind, even if only briefly, whether trafficking may be a relevant consideration. In cases where trafficking could possibly be relevant, regard should be had to the indicators of trafficking set out in the section below, to determine whether further investigation is warranted.

You might be dealing with someone now accused of an offence who has a relevant previous conviction. Where the prosecution applies to admit this as bad character, it may be helpful to take instructions on the circumstances of the old offence. If it arose as a result of trafficking, then, first of all, it may be distinguishable from the new offence, which may render it inadmissible, or at least may be a point to explain to the jury. Second, you may be in a position to advise on appeal.

You might be dealing with an immigration appeal or a deportation matter. This may particularly be the case where the deportation order followed the offence. Under section 3 of the Immigration Act 1971, section 32 of the UK Borders Act 2007, and Part 13 of the Immigration Rules, a person who receives a sentence of immediate (not suspended) imprisonment of 12 months or more will automatically receive a deportation order. The Secretary of State has a discretion to make a deportation order against those who have not received such a sentence, but whose offending has caused serious harm or who are persistent offenders who show a particular disregard for the law. Once made, a deportation order can be resisted with representations made based on the individual's human rights (often their family life and integration in the United Kingdom) or a risk of serious harm to them on return to their country of nationality. Deportation appeals are typically hard to win. It will almost always be worth considering whether the criminal conviction upon which the deportation order is based could be successfully appealed. If an appeal against conviction is successful, the deportation order will fall away.

In any of these cases, there may be "indicators of trafficking", which should make it easier to spot where a trafficking appeal may be advanced..

Indicators of trafficking

The Modern Slavery Statutory Guidance[108] sets out a number of indicators of trafficking, in particular that a victim may:

- Believe that they must work against their will;
- Be unable to leave their work environment or home environment;
- Show signs that their movements are being controlled;
- Feel that they cannot leave;

[108] 'Modern Slavery: Statutory Guidance for England and Wales (under S49 of the Modern Slavery Act 2015) and Non-Statutory Guidance for Scotland and Northern Ireland (Accessible Version)' (n 44) para 3.10.

- Show fear or anxiety;
- Have false identity or travel documents (or none at all);
- Be found in or connected to a type of location likely to be used for exploiting people;
- Be unfamiliar with the local language;
- Be subjected to violence or threats of violence against themselves or against their family members and loved ones;
- Suffer injuries that appear to be the result of an assault;
- Suffer injuries or impairments typical of certain jobs or control measures;
- Suffer injuries that appear to be the result of the application of control measures;
- Be distrustful of the authorities;
- Be threatened with being handed over to the authorities;
- Be afraid of revealing their immigration status;
- Not be in possession of their passports or other travel or identity documents, as those documents are being held by someone else;
- Come from a place known to be a source of human trafficking;
- Have had the fees for their transport to the country of destination paid for by facilitators, whom they must pay back by working or providing services in the destination;

- Not know their home or work address;
- Allow others to speak for them when addressed directly;
- Act as if they were instructed by someone else;
- Be forced, threatened or deceived into working in poor conditions;
- Be disciplined through punishment;
- Be unable to negotiate working conditions;
- Receive little or no payment;
- Have no access to their earnings;
- Work excessively long hours over long periods;
- Not have any days off;
- Live in poor or substandard accommodations;
- Have no access to medical care;
- Have limited or no social interaction;
- Have limited contact with their families or with people outside of their immediate environment;
- Be unable to communicate freely with others;
- Be under the perception that they are bonded by debt;
- Be in a situation of dependence;

- Have acted on the basis of false promises.

The Modern Slavery Statutory Guidance explicitly states that victims may "*be reluctant to come forward with information[;] not recognise themselves as having been trafficked or enslaved[; and] tell their stories with obvious errors and/or omissions*".[109]

The Modern Slavery Statutory Guidance also sets out a number of physical indicators (such as "*Gastrointestinal symptoms – abdominal pain or health conditions related to swallowed, internally placed or ruptured packets of illegal substances*" or "*Neurological symptoms – for example, headaches, dizzy spells, poor memory, poor concentration, problems with cognition, post traumatic epilepsy*" and of mental health conditions (such as "*an inability to regulate emotions*" and "*memory issues*").[110]

The Home Office collects anonymised data on the nationality of those referred into the NRM. Based on the current breakdown of referrals into the NRM, any case involving Albanian, Vietnamese, Eritrean, or Sudanese people may be disproportionately likely to involve trafficking.[111]

Common trafficking cases

In this section we set out some of the most common examples of trafficking cases, which can give rise to appeals. In practice, practitioners should be asking questions of any client who appears vulnerable (whether

---

[109] 'Modern Slavery: Statutory Guidance for England and Wales (under S49 of the Modern Slavery Act 2015) and Non-Statutory Guidance for Scotland and Northern Ireland (Accessible Version)' (n 44) para 3.6.

[110] 'Modern Slavery: Statutory Guidance for England and Wales (under S49 of the Modern Slavery Act 2015) and Non-Statutory Guidance for Scotland and Northern Ireland (Accessible Version)' (n 44) para 3.16.

[111] 'Modern Slavery: National Referral Mechanism and Duty to Notify Statistics UK, Quarter 3 2025 – July to September' (n 52).

that vulnerability is due to youth, mental health or neurodivergence, poverty, or irregular immigration status) and who has been convicted of a drug related offence, or an offence related to sex work.

The domestic production of drugs or their adulteration commonly involves the use of forced criminal exploitation in premises prepared for the purpose. Where a person has lived for any period in a facility producing drugs, forced criminal exploitation should be suspected. Victims of forced criminal exploitation in drug production related offences are commonly Vietnamese (particularly in cannabis production) or Albanian.

"Street level" drug dealing will also often be linked to forced criminal exploitation. The criminal legal system will tend to draw a distinction between people who agree to supply drugs in order to fund their own drug addiction, and those who are forced into drug dealing to pay off drug debts which dealers may have intentionally cultivated or inflated. Young British people, including children, may be particularly at risk.

Any vulnerable person convicted of an immigration related offence, including a false document offence, may be a victim of trafficking.

People, particularly women, involved in sex work may have found themselves in such a position because of trafficking. Offences which penalise those involved in sex work will disproportionately target those who are most economically marginalised and most at risk of exploitation. Offences such as solicitation (under section 1 of the Street Offences Act 1959) and keeping a brothel (under section 33A of the Sexual Offences Act 1956) may particularly target those who are forced into street sex work or sex work in exploitative brothel environments.

Financial offences where a victim appears to be under the coercive control of a partner may also involve a form of human trafficking. Such cases are often harder to locate, but may involve a person the victim thinks of as a "boyfriend" forcing them into the commission of acquisitive criminal offences.

CHAPTER EIGHT

APPEALING CONVICTIONS

Introduction

This chapter explains how appeals against conviction in trafficking cases work, and how they differ in practice to other appeals. It gives advice on how such appeals can be pursued most quickly and most effectively. The chapter is split into sections on appeals to the Crown Court and appeals to the Court of Appeal. It is followed by a short section on applications to the Criminal Cases Review Commission.

The right appeal in the right venue

The starting point is that the venue of appeal of a first-instance magistrates' or youth court decision is the Crown Court (or the High Court, if the appeal is by way of case stated or judicial review). The venue of appeal of a first-instance Crown Court decision is the Court of Appeal. However, a single case in the criminal courts can generate multiple parallel sets of proceedings. Where there has been a conviction in the magistrates' court followed by a committal for sentence, the same case may generate an appeal against conviction to the Crown Court and an appeal against sentence to the Court of Appeal. Equally, where there has been a guilty plea in the magistrates' court and a committal for sentence, the same case may generate an appeal against sentence to the Court of Appeal and an application to the Criminal Cases Review Commission for a referral of the conviction back to the Crown Court. As a result of the complexity of appeal routes that can arise, it is important to trace the precise procedural history of a case when beginning an appeal.

In trafficking appeals appellants may have particular difficulty accurately reporting their progress through the legal system due to a combination of youth, poor English language skills, unresolved trauma from their exploitation, and continuing trauma from their criminalisation. As a result, reliance on documentary materials and the accounts of appellants' previous lawyers will be particularly important in tracing the history of the case. Chapter 10 contains advice on navigating this difficulty.

Appeals to the Crown Court: convictions and guilty pleas in the adult magistrates' court and the youth court

Many victims of trafficking are convicted in the adult magistrates' courts or the youth court. A significant number of those convictions are guilty plea cases, which create issues for appeals, because under section 108(1) of the Magistrates' Court Act 1980, a person may only appeal against conviction to the Crown Court if they entered a not guilty plea.

Unless time is extended, then the time limit for an appeal to the Crown Court against conviction is 15 working days from the date of sentence, deferral of sentence, or committal for sentence, whichever is earlier.[112] If an application is made within that time then no leave to appeal is required. Outside that time, an application will need to be made for an extension of the time limit to appeal.[113] The application should set out the reasons that the appeal was late. Commonly this will be at least in part due to a delay in receiving the conclusive grounds decision. If the appeal follows a plea of guilty then the application should also include substantive grounds as to why the Crown Court has jurisdiction to hear the appeal: see further below.

---

[112] Criminal Procedure Rules, SI 2025/909 r 34.2.

[113] CrimPR r 34.3(a) & 34.10.

Appeals following not guilty pleas

Where a person has been convicted following trial in the magistrates' court or youth court, having pleaded not guilty throughout, appeal to the Crown Court is straightforward. The grounds of appeal served with the appeal notice should set out the grounds of appeal in very brief terms.

The Crown Court appeal will be a complete rehearing in front of a judge and two lay magistrates. That means that any issue of abuse of process can be revisited, and skeleton arguments should be refined and re-served. This should be raised at the mention to fix hearing and included in the time estimate for the appeal hearing.

Appeals following guilty pleas

There are many reasons why a defendant might plead guilty when a trafficking defence would be available to them.

Where victims of trafficking are subject to the trauma of trafficking, followed immediately by the trauma of arrest, and then remand overnight to court, there is no opportunity for them to reflect and recover from their trauma, and then to recount it to a lawyer in a way that could provide a defence.

In many cases, the victim of trafficking is not adequately advised about possible defences, either in the police station or at court. For this to stop being the case, frontline criminal defence practitioners will need to improve their understanding of the whole range of trafficking defences.

An appeal to the Crown Court *may still be available* even when a guilty plea has been recorded. This could be the case if (1) the guilty plea was equivocal or (2) the guilty plea was a nullity.

In these cases it is very common for there to have been a change of representative and for an appeal to be brought out of time. An application for an extension of time should be made on the appeal notice setting out the reasons for the delay.

The function of the Crown Court in these cases will be to investigate whether or not the plea was equivocal or a nullity, and if it was, to remit the matter to the magistrates' court or youth court for a fresh trial.[114] The Crown Court will not hear the fresh trial.

If the plea was not equivocal or a nullity then the Crown Court will not have jurisdiction. In those cases, the only option left is to make an application to the Criminal Cases Review Commission, or potentially the ECtHR.

Equivocal pleas

A plea may be equivocal at the time it is entered, such as when a defendant says "I'm guilty, but I was forced to do it". In those circumstances, following the proper procedure, the legal advisor ought to explain the law to the defendant and then re-take the plea. If the plea remains equivocal, then a not guilty plea should be entered on the defendant's behalf. If that procedure was not followed, an appeal should be made to the Crown Court

Alternatively, and as may be more common in cases such as this, a plea may subsequently be shown to be equivocal. This will be the case where material emerges in mitigation at sentence which undermines the guilty plea.[115] It is often tempting to rely exclusively on material from third

[114] *Phillips v Isleworth Crown Court* [2023] EWHC 617 (Admin), [2023] 2 Cr App R 8 [25–28]; *R (on the application of the Crown Prosecution Service) v Crown Court at Preston* [2023] EWHC 1957 (Admin), [2024] KB 348.

[115] *R (on the application of the Crown Prosecution Service) v Crown Court at Preston* (n 114) paras 29–31; *Dumitru Palazu, R v* [2020] EWCA Crim 1627 [27–29]; *R v Durham Quarter Sessions ex parte Virgo* [1952] 2 QB 1; *R v Blandford Justices ex parte G* [1967] 1 QB 82.

parties, such as a conclusive grounds decision, social worker assessments, or pre-sentence reports. However, practitioners should be aware that in an appeal of this nature, it is very likely that privilege will need to be waived and attendance notes of the client's instructions at the time of the plea produced. Where the client has given clear guilty instructions at the time, the court may find that the plea was unequivocal, notwithstanding third-party material undermining the plea. It will be essential to take the client's clear instructions as to whether or not a possible defence was discussed, and, if it was not, why not. The client may need to be tendered to give evidence of these matters before the Crown Court.

Pleas which are a nullity

Where a Defendant enters a guilty plea, and it is established that incorrect legal advice was given such that the plea was not a true acknowledgement of guilt, that plea will be a nullity.[116] This will be the case where "the appellant was deprived of what was, in all likelihood, a good defence in law".[117]

Appeals to the Court of Appeal: convictions and guilty pleas in the Crown Court

Procedure

Those who are convicted or plead guilty in the Crown Court have a right of appeal to the Court of Appeal. All applicants must apply for leave to appeal, but in practical terms the application for leave will be the same as the grounds of appeal themselves. The application for leave to appeal will be considered by a single judge on the papers. If leave is granted on the papers then a representation order will be granted for counsel to appear at an oral hearing of the appeal in the Court of Appeal heard by three

116 *R (on the application of Golrokhi) v Chelmsford Crown Court* [2013] EWHC 4343 (Admin) [27–31].

117 *Boal, R v* [1992] QB 591.

judges. If leave is not granted on the papers then the application can be renewed orally in the Court of Appeal, but there will be no representation order and so generally speaking no funding for counsel.

In legally aided cases, there is generally no funding for grounds of appeal to be drafted by trial counsel because the funding for grounds of appeal is said to be included in the brief fee. However, where trial counsel has advised negatively on appeal, funding may be available for a second opinion from different counsel.

The time limit for an application for leave to appeal to the Court of Appeal is 28 days from the date of the order being appealed, whether that be conviction or sentence.[118] That period may be extended at the discretion of the Registrar, the single judge, or the full court.[119] The application for leave to appeal must include details as to the reason for the delay, as good reason will generally be required.[120] A delay in obtaining a conclusive grounds decision will generally be a good reason, although any other periods of delay will need to be well explained.

In cases where the merits of an appeal are good, the Court of Appeal may grant an extension of time to appeal even where there is no good reason for the delay because, if the appeal has merit, the refusal may lead to a reference to the Criminal Cases Review Commission, for which there is no time limit.[121]

---

[118] Criminal Appeal Act 1968 s 18.

[119] Criminal Appeal Act 1968 s 18(3).

[120] *Wilson, R v* [2016] EWCA Crim 65.

[121] *King, R v* [2000] 2 Cr App R 391.

Grounds of appeal

The Court of Appeal's power to overturn a conviction is found in section 2 of the Criminal Appeal Act 1968, which provides that the single test for an appeal against conviction is whether the conviction is "unsafe".

A verdict may be unsafe where, for example, evidence was incorrectly admitted or excluded, where the judge misdirected the jury as to law in summing up, or where new evidence previously unavailable is now available.

Most commonly, grounds of appeal will arise where, after conviction, there has been a positive conclusive grounds decision, or a finding of fact in another court that the defendant was a victim of trafficking and that the offence arose out of that trafficking.[122] The decision of a Judge of the First-tier Tribunal or the Competent Authority is not binding upon the Court of Appeal but in the absence of evidence which undermines it, it is likely that the criminal courts will abide by that decision.[123] In this context, a conviction is unsafe if the circumstances are sufficient to reduce the appellant's culpability below a point where it is in the public interest to prosecute, or, in other words, the appellant would, or might well, not have been prosecuted if the true position had been known.[124]

Grounds should set out in detail the background to the case, the legal framework around non-prosecution and non-punishment of victims of trafficking and the Crown Prosecution Service guidance and 4 stage test (see Chapter 4 and Chapter 5). They should include close analysis of the conclusive grounds decision or of the facts found by the other court to

---

122 *AFU, R v* (n 81) para 136.

123 *VSJ, R v* [2017] EWCA Crim 36, [2017] 1 WLR 3153 [20]; *O, R v* [2019] EWCA Crim 1389 [18].

124 *GS, R v* [2018] EWCA Crim 1824, [2019] 1 Cr App R 7 [76(v)]; *BXR, R v* [2022] EWCA Crim 1483 [16, 47]; *AAC, R v* [2023] EWCA Crim 15 [36, 46].

show why, had the prosecution been aware of the fresh evidence and applied their guidance, they would have discontinued proceedings either on the evidential or public interest limbs of the test, or alternatively proceedings would have been stayed (see Chapter 5).

Particularly close attention should be paid to the nexus between the trafficking and the offence, and the absence of reasonable alternatives (issues which are often elided), as difficulties in these areas often lead to the refusal of criminal appeals.[125]

Particularly close attention should also be paid to the reliability of the conclusive grounds decision. In cases where the conclusive grounds decision is based only or mainly on the appellant's account, the court has declined to find it credible. In those cases the appellant should generally be called to give evidence at the Court of Appeal.[126] In *BNN* the prosecution argued that the conclusive grounds decision was based only on the appellant's account, which was not particularly detailed. They sought to cross-examine the appellant on matters going to the offence and to his plea. The appellant's counsel argued that it would be unnecessary for him to give evidence, and also detrimental to his wellbeing, although there was no finding that he was unfit.[127] He was not tendered, and the Court of Appeal dismissed the appeal, finding that his evidence of being trafficked was "*unsatisfactory and untested*" and that "*we draw no adverse inference from this refusal but are obviously unable to obtain clarification of lacunae or apparent inconsistencies in his account to assist our consideration of the submissions made on his behalf.*"[128] Conversely in *BSG*, where a First-tier Tribunal had heard evidence from the appellant on matters which "substantially overlapped" with those before the Court of

[125] See e.g. *BLS, R v* [2022] EWCA Crim 1079; *AUL, R v* [2022] EWCA Crim 1435; *BRP, R v* [2023] EWCA Crim 40; *BNN, R v* (n 72).

[126] *AAD, AAH, and AAI, R v* (n 15) para 108.

[127] *BNN, R v* (n 72) para 52.

[128] *BNN, R v* (n 72) paras 53–54.

Appeal and found him to be credible, submissions that he should not be tendered to give evidence were accepted, even though there was evidence which might have undermined his account.[129]

Grounds should also identify whether there was any point in the proceedings below when the police failed to refer the appellant into the NRM, where the prosecution failed to make relevant enquiries, or where the judge failed to make enquiries and either adjourn the case pending the result of the NRM referral or stay it.[130]

Appealing in the Court of Appeal after a guilty plea

A conviction may be rendered unsafe by a subsequent conclusive grounds decision or other further evidence, even where a defendant pleaded guilty at trial.[131]

There are three categories of case in which a conviction may be unsafe despite a guilty plea.[132]

The first category is **cases where the guilty plea is vitiated.** This can occur in a number of scenarios. For example, the conviction of an appellant who was under the influence of controlled drugs when they entered their guilty plea could not be said to be safe.[133] Equally, a plea may have been compelled by an adverse or incorrect ruling as to the law (for example, that a particular defence was not available).[134] In the same vein, there may have been improper pressure applied to the appellant, for example

---

[129] *BSG, R v* [2023] EWCA Crim 1041 [52–55].

[130] *N, R v* [2019] EWCA Crim 984 [40].

[131] *AAD, AAH, and AAI, R v* (n 15) para 155; *AFU, R v* (n 81).

[132] *Boal, R v* (n 117); *Tredget, R v* [2022] EWCA Crim 108, [2022] 4 WLR 62 [154–180].

[133] *Swain, R v* [1986] Crim LR 480.

[134] *Asiedu, R v* [2015] EWCA Crim 714, [2015] 2 Cr App R 8 [20].

where an indication of likely sentence is given without being requested.[135] Finally, incorrect legal advice may have deprived the appellant of a defence which quite probably would have succeeded such that a clear injustice has been done.[136]

The second category is **cases where there was a legal obstacle to the appellant being tried**. This will be the case where the prosecution should have been stayed on grounds that it was an abuse of process to prosecute the appellant. In such cases, "By parity of reasoning, if the trial process should never have taken place because it is offensive to justice, a conviction upon a guilty plea is as unsafe as one following trial".[137]

The third category is **cases where the admission made by the plea is a false one**, because it is established the appellant did not commit the offence.[138]

When arguing that a guilty plea has been vitiated by incorrect legal advice, or by improper pressure applied by counsel, legal privilege will need to be waived. The appellant will need to provide a witness statement setting out what they can remember about the circumstances of their conferences with their representatives and advice they received. As with any appeal, the previous representative will need to be contacted to give their views. In this sort of case, the previous representative will need to provide their attendance notes along with any further explanation of their memory of what they advised. Where there is a dispute as to what was advised, both the appellant and the previous representative may be called to give oral evidence in the Court of Appeal.[139] Where the appellant

---

135 *Nightingale, R v* [2013] EWCA Crim 405, [2013] 2 Cr App R 7.

136 *Boal, R v* (n 117).

137 *Asiedu, R v* (n 134) para 21.

138 *Verney, R v* (1909) 2 Cr App R 107; *Foster, R v* [1985] QB 115.

139 *AFU, R v* (n 81) para 122.

declines in those circumstances to give evidence, the court has found this ground of appeal to be unarguable.[140]

The test the Court will apply when considering whether a failure to advise an appellant about the availability of the defence under section 45 of the Modern Slavery Act 2015 is whether it probably would have succeeded. That test was divided into 4 parts in *R v Dastjerdi*.[141] Firstly, that the appellant should have been advised about the possibility of availing themselves of the section 45 defence; secondly, that the appellant was not so advised; thirdly, that, had the appellant been so advised, it was open to them to advance the defence; and fourthly that the prospects that the appellant would have been able successfully to advance such a defence were good.

In both *R v BLS*[142] and *R v BRP*,[143] it was accepted that the defence advocate at trial had not advised the appellant about the availability of the section 45 defence. However, the Court of Appeal held that the defence would not probably have succeeded, because the appellant had a realistic alternative to complying with the demands of the traffickers. In *R v BLS* the Court of Appeal expressed this as "*there was no nexus between the applicant's being trafficked into the UK and his carrying out his function as a cannabis gardener... [because] by the time of his arrest the applicant was not the subject of compulsion.*" In *obiter* comments in *BRP*, the Court took into account factors pointing towards and away from the appellant's credibility, stepping into the shoes of the fact finder.[144] Although not admissible at trial, it took into account the conclusive grounds decision as evidence pointing towards the Appellant's credibility. However the *ratio* of the decision was that "*even accepting his account for present*

140 *BNN, R v* (n 72) paras 56, 60.

141 *Dastjerdi (Bakhshi Ali), R v* [2011] EWCA Crim 365 [9].

142 *BLS, R v* (n 125).

143 *BRP, R v* (n 125).

144 *BRP, R v* (n 125) paras 61–62.

purposes, we consider it clear that the prosecution would have been likely to prove to the criminal standard of proof that at least one of the necessary ingredients of a s. 45 defence was not made out."[145]

In contrast, for a successful application of this ground see *R v BSG*.[146]

Even where the guilty plea was not vitiated, for example where the appellant decided to plead guilty despite legal advice that a defence was available, or where there genuinely was no defence because the offence fell under Schedule 4 of the Modern Slavery Act 2014, it still may have been an abuse of process to try the appellant *in the light of fresh evidence.* As such, appeal cases should always be considered holistically, with attention being paid to all possible ways the case could have been defended at trial if all relevant evidence had then been available.

Applications to the Criminal Cases Review Commission

The Criminal Appeal Act 1995 sets out the powers of the Criminal Cases Review Commission ("**CCRC**"). When there has already been an unsuccessful appeal, the CCRC can refer cases back to the Crown Court or Court of Appeal for another appeal to take place. When a person has pleaded guilty in the magistrates' court the CCRC can also refer cases back to the Crown Court for an appeal to take place. This possibility of referring guilty plea cases back to the Crown Court remains available even where the guilty plea was not equivocal or a nullity.

In determining an application, the CCRC will consider a 3-part test:[147]

1. Unless there are exceptional circumstances, the CCRC can only refer a case for an appeal if there has been a previous appeal. In

[145] *BRP, R v* (n 125) para 63.

[146] *BSG, R v* (n 129) paras 49–57.

[147] Criminal Appeal Act 1995 s 13.

cases where there was a guilty plea in the magistrates' court "*there will always be potential exceptional circumstances*".[148]

2. The CCRC can only refer any case if "*there is a real possibility that the conviction, verdict, finding or sentence would not be upheld*" i.e. a real possibility that the conviction would be found unsafe, or that the sentence would be found to be manifestly excessive or wrong in principle.

3. Unless there are exceptional circumstances, it can only refer a conviction because of new arguments or information. Even if there are exceptional circumstances, it can only refer a sentence because of new arguments or information.

148 Criminal Cases Review Commission, 'Casework Policy: Exceptional Circumstances CW-POL-06' para 3.2.

CHAPTER NINE

APPEALING SENTENCES

Introduction

As set out in Chapter 8, the first step in dealing with an appeal case is to work out the correct venue for the appeal.

Where the sentence was in a magistrates' court or youth court, the appeal will usually be to the Crown Court. The time limit is 15 business days from the date of sentence and may be extended (see Chapter 8). As with an appeal against conviction, there is no need to apply for leave to appeal or to advance particular grounds of appeal; rather the appeal will be a rehearing of the original sentencing exercise. If the sentence is not reduced on appeal, the prosecution will apply for costs, currently £705, which the court has a discretion to impose taking into account the appellant's means.[149]

Where the sentence was in the Crown Court, the appeal against sentence will be to the Court of Appeal. The time limit is 28 days from the date of sentence, and may be extended (see Chapter 8). An application for leave to appeal will need to be made, the procedure for which is the same as for appeal against conviction to the Court of Appeal. The grounds of appeal may only be that the sentence was manifestly excessive, or that the sentence was wrong in principle.

---

[149] Crown Prosecution Service, 'Costs – Annex 1' (30 April 2024) <https://www.cps.gov.uk/prosecution-guidance/costs-annex-1> accessed 12 December 2025.

Where an appeal has already taken place, or an application for leave to appeal was made and refused, an application will need to be made to the Criminal Cases Review Commission.

The basis for an appeal against sentence

The fact that someone has committed an offence as a result of exploitation will often be a specific factor reducing culpability on the sentencing guidelines, thus bringing the starting point down. Even if it is not, the argument should be made as it is obvious: someone who is following directions under some form of coercion is less culpable than someone giving the directions.

Where a survivor of trafficking is sentenced for a matter which does not result from their trafficking experience, their experience should still be a mitigating feature.[150] They may, for example, have mental health difficulties which flow from their experiences. Further and in the alternative, the argument can simply be made that they have suffered a lot in life.

Further, the value to an appellant of an appeal against sentence can be relevant to the basis of the appeal itself, as it may be determinative of whether the sentence was manifestly excessive when all information which is now available is considered.

The value of an appeal against sentence

The Court of Appeal is slow. Many appellants only have their cases heard well after their sentences are complete. Where sentences are reduced on appeal, a person will receive no apology, let alone compensation, for the time they wrongly spent in prison up to the date of their appeal being determined. Appellants may therefore wonder what the point of an appeal against sentence could be if they have already completed their

---

[150] *AAD, AAH, and AAI, R v* (n 15) para 169.

sentence. There are several such reasons, which may be cited as being relevant to grounds of appeal against sentence.

Firstly, **deportation**. People who are not British citizens and who receive criminal convictions may become liable to deportation. Different legal regimes apply to people who were not sent to prison or who had short prison sentences; people who received prison sentences of at least a year but less than 4 years; and people who received prison sentences of at least 4 years. Those with longer prison sentences are significantly more likely to be deported than those with shorter prison sentences or who serve non-custodial sentences.

Secondly, **citizenship applications**. Those who have criminal convictions may be permanently ineligible for citizenship, depending on the sentence received. The law on the good character requirement for citizenship is constantly evolving. At the time of writing, under section 58 of the Immigration, Asylum and Nationality Act 2006 a person can be barred for life from acquiring British citizenship if they have received certain types of sentences. Home Office guidance provides more information on what types of conviction and sentence will amount to an obstacle to a grant of citizenship, and for how long such an obstacle will remain in place.

Thirdly, **spent convictions**. The legal provisions on the rehabilitation of offenders are designed to make sure that people who are convicted of criminal offences do not have to disclose them for their whole lives. After a period of time most criminal convictions become "spent". A person whose conviction is spent may be treated as being of good character, and may not need to disclose their conviction when applying for jobs, purchasing, insurance, or at other times. The length and seriousness of a sentence determines when the conviction becomes spent.

Fourthly, **disclosure and barring**. A person who receives a criminal conviction may not automatically have that conviction disclosed by the Disclosure and Barring Service when applying for certain types of jobs. A conviction which was dealt with by the imposition of a lower level of sentence may not be disclosed, whereas the same conviction which was dealt with by the imposition of a more severe sentence may be disclosed.

Fifthly, **fair labelling**. Society, and people with convictions, are entitled to see that convictions are marked with appropriate penalties. The principle of fair labelling requires that no higher a sentence is passed on someone than necessary to mark the severity of their offending. For some appellants, fair labelling may be an important matter for their own self-esteem, as being a person who it was considered legally right to subject to a serious criminal penalty may be a mark of shame.

Sixthly, **the impact on sentencing for further offending**. The existence of previous convictions is a relevant aggravating factor in sentencing. As a result, if a person is subsequently convicted of further offences then they will usually be dealt with more harshly than they would be dealt with for a first offence. If a person was previously subject to a sentence of imprisonment, then a sentencing judge may think be more inclined to sentence them to imprisonment again, and to impose a longer term of imprisonment than previously.

Ultimately, as the Office of the Special Representative and Co-ordinator for Combating Trafficking in Human Beings at the Organization for Security and Co-operation in Europe has noted in her 2013 report:

> "In the situation where a person has been trafficked and is therefore unable to act with free will, even an unpenalized conviction is in fact a punishment. The mere existence of a conviction is in itself a punishment and may have negative consequences for the victim in future because they would have a criminal record, and as a result might be restricted from certain activities, including limitations to their freedom

> of movement (e.g., not permitted to travel to another country) or to access certain employment."[151]

While a successful appeal against sentence alone will not remove the stain of conviction referred to above, it may nonetheless remove some of these continuing consequences of conviction.

---

[151] Office of the Special Representative and Co-ordinator for Combating Trafficking in Human Beings (n 39) para 77.

CHAPTER TEN

CONSIDERATIONS IN ALL APPEALS

Fresh evidence in appeals

Fresh evidence in Crown Court appeals

An appeal in the Crown Court is a retrial, and there is generally no restriction on fresh evidence being adduced.

In respect of any evidence which would have needed to be accompanied by an application or prior notice at the lower court (including hearsay and expert opinion evidence) an application should be made or notice given in the same terms as it would have been in the lower court not more than 14 days after the service of the appeal notice.[152] Strictly speaking, this would not apply to a fresh conclusive grounds decision intended for use in an application to stay, although this should in any event be provided along with representations to discontinue as soon as possible. Providing material early will allow the prosecution time to consider whether or not to contest the appeal, and to provide reasons for continuing if it will be contested.

Fresh evidence in appeals to the Court of Appeal

Under section 23 of the Criminal Appeal Act 1968, the Court of Appeal may, if they think it necessary or expedient in the interests of justice, admit fresh evidence which was not considered at trial, if it "appears necessary for the determination of the case". Under section 23(2), the

[152] CrimPR r 34.7.

Court shall "*have regard in particular to (a) whether the evidence appears to the court to be capable of belief; (b) whether it appears to the Court that the evidence may afford any ground for allowing the appeal; (c) whether the evidence would have been admissible in the proceedings from which the appeal lies on an issue which is the subject of the appeal; and (d) whether there is a reasonable explanation for the failure to adduce the evidence in those proceedings.*"

Fresh evidence which was not available at trial and which the prosecution would have needed to take into account when applying the 4-stage test will generally be admissible. Therefore, although not admissible at trial, a fresh conclusive grounds decision is generally admissible at appeal as relevant to the determination of whether it was an abuse of process to try the appellant.[153] Similarly a subsequent decision by another court in which it was found as fact that the appellant was trafficked, a subsequent medical report, or a subsequent asylum interview which would have needed to have been taken into account in deciding whether to prosecute, will generally be admissible.[154]

Evidence which was available at trial but overlooked could be admissible, particularly where the appellant was not consulted.[155]

In all fresh evidence cases consideration should be given to waiver of privilege, as explained further below.

Explaining delay

In any case where the time limit to appeal has already expired, the representatives will need to explain the delay in filing the appeal.

---

[153] *AAD, AAH, and AAI, R v* (n 15) para 81.

[154] *N, R v* (n 130) paras 6–8.

[155] *Ahluwalia, R v* (1993) 96 Cr App R 133.

In some very old cases, there may have been a change in the law or practice to bring the United Kingdom's domestic law into line with its international obligations. This would be the case for instance in cases dating from before the introduction of CPS policies governing the non-prosecution of victims of trafficking, or from before the modern caselaw on non-liability obligations.

In many cases, appellants will have been psychologically unable to disclose the trafficking situation at an earlier date. In particular, where appellants have immediately been subject to the trauma of criminalisation at the conclusion of their trafficking experiences, they may not have been psychologically capable of making appropriate disclosures, either to the police or their own representatives. As a result, the traumatisation of the prosecution process may itself be the cause of the delay in disclosure. It would be odd for the state to say that delay, caused by the trauma occasioned by its own actions in defiance of its international obligations to identify and protect victims of trafficking, could justify either refusing an extension of time to appeal, or the taking of a critical stance towards the late disclosure.

The Modern Slavery Statutory Guidance explains how delays in disclosure may occur. It notes in particular that "*Victims' early accounts may be affected by the impact of trauma. This can result in delayed disclosure, difficulty recalling facts, or symptoms of post-traumatic stress disorder. Victims may also be reluctant to self-identify for a number of other reasons that can make understanding their experiences challenging.*"[156] Regard should be had to what is said in the Statutory Guidance when drafting any application for an extension of time.

---

156 'Modern Slavery: Statutory Guidance for England and Wales (under S49 of the Modern Slavery Act 2015) and Non-Statutory Guidance for Scotland and Northern Ireland (Accessible Version)' (n 44) para 13.1.

Obviously, not every case where there is delay in filing an appeal will be explained by factors relating to delayed disclosure. Often delay will be due to a failure of representatives to properly take instructions or advise.

In order to justify any extension of time, full instructions will need to be taken from the appellant, usually supported by a witness statement from the solicitor. If this is filed with the Court of Appeal, then it should have Form W as a cover. The timeline of the receipt of instructions to appeal, how those instructions came about, and subsequent steps by the representatives should also be explained.

Contacting previous representatives

When a victim of trafficking is convicted, they may try to challenge their conviction by criticising the conduct of their defence by their trial lawyers. Criticism of trial lawyers can make it inappropriate for the trial lawyers to continue to represent the victim of trafficking at an appeal. Equally, trial lawyers may realise that they failed to properly advise a victim of trafficking on the defences available to them, and they may feel that they have to withdraw from the case and refer the victim of trafficking to new lawyers. In other cases, a victim of trafficking may only realise that they could appeal against a conviction or sentence years later, when they have no ongoing relationship with their trial lawyers. In any of these eventualities, new lawyers will need to be instructed to take on the case.

The McCook duty in the Court of Appeal

When they take on an appeal, new lawyers have specific duties to the court and to their client. In the case of *R v McCook*[157] the Court of Appeal began a process of imposing increasingly strict guidelines on new lawyers. They held that when fresh lawyers are instructed for an appeal they must approach the previous lawyers "*to ensure that the facts are correct, unless*

[157] *McCook, R v* [2014] EWCA Crim 734, [2016] 2 Cr App R 30.

there are in exceptional circumstances good and compelling reasons not to do so." This has come to be known as the "McCook duty".

In *R v Grant-Murray*[158] the Court of Appeal held that the McCook duty is not complied with simply by sending the grounds of appeal to trial lawyers and asking for comments. Instead, specific questions must be formulated and there must be no shying away from putting any criticism of the trial lawyers. Subsequently, in *R v James*[159] the Court of Appeal clarified that after the trial lawyers have responded to enquiries, fresh lawyers must consider whether the grounds of appeal are properly arguable. If they are not properly arguable then an application must not be made to the Court of Appeal.

The Criminal Practice Directions 2023 provide detail on how to comply with the McCook duty. New legal representatives must state within the grounds of appeal that the *McCook* duty has been complied with.[160] A signed waiver of privilege is required where privileged information is included, particularly where complaints are made about trial representatives.[161] In practice where there are criticisms of trial representatives the Court of Appeal Office will often write directly to the fresh lawyers and the appellant in order to obtain a waiver of privilege. If there is no response from the trial representatives then fresh lawyers must file a statement confirming this.[162] If the trial representatives do not respond or if the trial representatives contradict the appellant, then the fresh lawyers must seek other objective independent evidence to

---

158 *Grant-Murray, R v* [2017] EWCA Crim 1228.

159 *James, R v* [2018] EWCA Crim 285, [2018] 1 WLR 2749.

160 Criminal Practice Directions 2023 para 10.4.4(a).

161 Criminal Practice Directions 2023 para 10.4.4(b).

162 Criminal Practice Directions 2023 para 10.4.4(c).

substantiate the factual basis of the appeal.[163] Waiver of privilege is considered further in the section below.

When fresh representatives write to trial representatives it may be helpful to explain the explicit extent of the trial lawyers' obligations. Responding to inquiries under the McCook duty is not an opportunity for trial lawyers to express their personal opinions about the appellant's guilt, the weight of the evidence against them, or any other matter. Trial representatives should be asked to limit themselves to responding to specific questions about whether the factual basis of the proposed appeal is correct, and to factually address any specific alleged failings in their own conduct. In particular, in trafficking cases where it is said that inadequate advice was given as to the availability of trafficking defences, trial lawyers should be asked (1) what information they had relevant to whether the applicant was a potential victim of trafficking; and (2) what advice they gave about possible trafficking defences. The specific questions that should be asked will vary from case to case based on the instructions provided by the appellant.

A McCook duty in the Crown Court and Criminal Cases Review Commission?

Neither the Criminal Practice Directions nor caselaw set out an equivalent McCook duty in the Crown Court. However, new lawyers would still be well-advised to comply with the McCook duty on an appeal to the Crown Court. Although the McCook duty is framed in a coercive way by the Court of Appeal, it can nonetheless be seen as a positive set of reminders for fresh lawyers. Advancing an inarguable case or a case based on incorrect information benefits no one: it is a waste of time, resources, and hope. In the absence of exceptional circumstances, there can be no good reason not to comply with the McCook duty. Further, a failure to do in the Crown Court what the McCook duty

[163] Criminal Practice Directions 2023 para 10.4.4(c) & (d).

would require in the Court of Appeal can still lead to costs and professional sanctions, as set out below.

Matters are more complicated in applications to the Criminal Cases Review Commission ("CCRC"). The CCRC is not a court, and so the same set of obligations cannot directly apply in applications to it. However, if a case is referred by the CCRC to an appellate court then the enquiries which form the basis of the McCook duty would still need to be made. Either they would be made by the CCRC, or the fresh representatives would need to make them, or the Court of Appeal Office may initiate the enquiries itself. In all of these circumstances, it is possible that information may come to light which shows that the factual basis of an application was inaccurate. Once again, advancing an inarguable case or a case based on incorrect information benefits no one.

Waiver of privilege

In recent years, the Court of Appeal has taken an increasingly strict approach to requiring waiver of legal privilege by appellants, particularly in cases where fresh evidence is to be adduced in an appeal. Lady Justice Hallett, the then-Vice-President of the Court of Appeal (Criminal Division) complained about applications to rely on fresh evidence becoming "increasingly prevalent" and "taking up a considerable amount of the limited time and resources available" to the Court of Appeal, and this appeared to justify a stricter approach.[164] Unfortunately, no statistical evidence was provided in support of this complaint.

The consequence of this approach is that representatives should fully advise clients and take detailed instructions on whether legal privilege can be waived in all appeal cases. Where there are criticisms of trial representatives then waiver of privilege will usually be necessary. Further, where there is new evidence to be relied upon, there may need to be a waiver of privilege so that it can be explained why the evidence was not

[164] *Singh (Kunwar), R v* [2017] EWCA Crim 466, [2018] 1 WLR 1425 [49].

available at trial. This includes cases where the new evidence is relevant to whether the proceedings were an abuse of process. The Criminal Practice Direction states that in the Court of Appeal a waiver of privilege is required "in all fresh evidence cases".[165]

Clients may worry about the implication of waiver of privilege, and there is a natural hesitancy on the part of representatives to advise in favour of waiving privilege. However, where a person has already been convicted the worst that could happen from a waiver of privilege – losing the case to which the privilege relates – has already happened. The harm of waiver of privilege needs to be balanced against the Court of Appeal's approach of criticising appellants who do not waive privilege and, in some cases, asserting that they are unable to determine whether complaints constitute an arguable ground of appeal without a waiver of privilege.[166]

In any case where there is a waiver of privilege, the waiver should identify clearly the areas over which privilege is waived. The principle of collateral waiver means that the waiver will apply not just to specific documents relied upon, but to all material relevant to the same issue.[167]

Anonymity

Orders which anonymise appellants in the Court of Appeal may be available in appeals for victims of trafficking. However, the starting point is the importance of the principle of open justice, and anonymity orders can only be justified when they are strictly necessary on the facts of the case. The Court of Appeal will balance the rights of the appellant to anonymity against the rights of others to open justice. The court may grant a withholding order (an order which permits or directs the withholding of the name of the appellant and replacing it with a cipher

[165] Criminal Practice Directions 2023 para 10.4.4(e).

[166] *Frost-Helmsing (Anthony), R* [2010] EWCA Crim 1200 [14–15].

[167] *Nea Karteria Maritime Co v Atlantic and Great Lakes Steamship Corp (No2)* [1981] Com LR 138 139.

such as AAA) and a reporting restriction order (an order prohibiting publication of the withheld name or any other information that would be likely to identify the person whom the court has directed should be anonymised). A withholding order will prevent a party's name from being made public as a result of the proceedings, but will not in itself prevent the party being publicly identified if their identity is already known or can be discovered. An application for a withholding order is therefore usually coupled with an application for a reporting restriction order.[168]

The Court of Appeal had adopted a general approach of anonymising the appellant in cases raising issues related to asylum, but has noted that there are also contrary considerations, and that there may be less restrictive means than anonymity to address the risk of harm that could arise from appellants' names being publicised.[169] Recent case law may suggest that the Court of Appeal is becoming more hesitant to take the approach of anonymising appellants who have also raised issues related to asylum.[170] Nonetheless, where an appellant's rights under Articles 2 or 3 of the ECHR are engaged by the decision to name them, because there could be reprisals from the traffickers, that will usually be determinative of an application for anonymity. This will be the case where, for example, the appellant has given details of their trafficking, traffickers, or their place of origin.[171] This will also be the case where those rights are only potentially engaged, because the relevant issues have not yet been determined.[172]

Further, where another court or tribunal, such as the First-tier Tribunal (Immigration and Asylum Chamber) or the Administrative Court, has

---

[168] *Baniulyte, R v* [2025] EWCA (Crim) 1205.

[169] *L & N, R v* [2017] EWCA Crim 2129 [15].

[170] *Baniulyte, R v* (n 168).

[171] *L & N, R v* (n 169) para 33.

[172] *AAD, AAH, and AAI, R v* (n 15) para 184.

made an anonymity direction, the Court of Appeal may find that to not continue the grant of anonymity would undermine the orders of the other court.[173]

An application for anonymity will need to comply with the requirements of the Criminal Procedure Rules 2025 rule 6.4. An application must be made as soon as reasonably practicable (usually when the appeal is lodged); on notice to all other parties and reporters; specifying the proposed terms of the order and for how long it should last; and explaining what power the court has to make the order (usually section 11 of the Contempt of Court Act 1981) and why an order in the terms proposed is necessary. The application should be supported by evidence, including evidence of the risk of harm if anonymity is not granted, and details of any grant of anonymity made by any other court or tribunal.[174]

The Court of Appeal may list a case under a cipher and make a withholding order and a reporting restrictions order on a temporary basis, pending judgment or further order. Advocates should attend any hearing fully prepared to address the issue of whether orders anonymising the appellant should be continued, as the court may want to hear detailed evidence on the issue.

Sanctions for unmeritorious applications and failure to comply with duties

Sanctions can be imposed on lawyers and appellants where frivolous or vexatious applications are made to the Court of Appeal.

Loss of time orders against applicants

If an applicant to the Court of Appeal is in custody then the Court of Appeal can consider making a "loss of time order" if they are

[173] *AAD, AAH, and AAI, R v* (n 15) para 52.

[174] *Baniulyte, R v* (n 168) para 111.

unsuccessful.[175] A loss of time order means that some time spent in prison waiting for the appeal to be heard does not count towards the sentence. That means spending longer in prison. Usually this is a period of 2-6 weeks. The loss of time order can technically relate to the entire sentence, but we have never heard of a loss of time order exceeding 6 weeks.

A loss of time order cannot be imposed where permission to appeal is granted, where an appeal was referred to the Court of Appeal by the Criminal Cases Review Commission, or where a certificate was granted by the judge who dealt with the matter being appealed against.[176] It is the practice of the Court of Appeal not to impose a loss of time order simply for making an application to the single judge for permission to appeal.[177] As a result, a loss of time order will only be made following a refusal of permission on the papers and oral renewal.

The Single Judge dealing with the application on the papers may "*initial the box*" on the form refusing permission to appeal, if they consider that the appeal is totally without merit.

If an application for oral renewal is made, and the Full Court refuses permission to appeal, it may consider making a loss of time order. It will *always* consider making a loss of time order if the Single Judge "*initialled the box*". It may still impose a loss of time order even if the Single Judge did not give a direction that imposing one should be considered, and even if an applicant was advised by lawyers to continue with their application.[178]

---

[175] Criminal Appeal Act 1968 s 29.

[176] Criminal Appeal Act 1968 s 29(2).

[177] 'Guide to Proceedings in the Court of Appeal, Criminal Division' para C.5.1.

[178] *Fortean, R v* [2009] EWCA Crim 437.

In *R v Gray*[179] Lady Justice Hallett on behalf of the Court of Appeal set out a statement of principle about how unmeritorious applications should be dealt with. She stated that "*The only means the Court has of discouraging unmeritorious applications which waste precious time and resources is by using the powers*" to make loss of time orders and costs orders. The Court of Appeal based the need to discourage unmeritorious applications on the weight of work that the Court of Appeal had to consider, and the backlogs that resulted from this. However, in reaching this conclusion the Court of Appeal did not attempt to analyse the number of unmeritorious applications made to it, and whether these in fact contributed to the backlog in dealing with appeals. Nor did it consider whether there might be other causes, such as systematic lack of funding for the court system arising out of deliberate austerity policies. Nor did it consider whether there was any evidence that loss of time orders were capable of preventing unmeritorious applications. Equally, it did not consider whether its actions in imposing loss of time orders may have a chilling effect on the right to appeal, discouraging people from pursuing applications that could ultimately be meritorious. In the case of *R v Gray*, in which the Court of Appeal set out their view that a stricter approach needed to be taken to unmeritorious applications, the Court of Appeal had based that conclusion on there being 6,500 applications per year to the Court of Appeal in 2013-2014. However, that was significantly less than in 1969, in which there were 9,700 applications. In 1970 the Court of Appeal sought to clamp down on unmeritorious applications by using loss of time orders similarly to how they later did in *R v Gray*,[180] following which applications fell to approximately 500 per month.[181] The fact that the number of applications in 2014 was not significantly different to the number in 1970 despite a rise in the

---

[179] *Gray, R v* [2014] EWCA Crim 2372, [2015] 1 Cr App R (S) 27.

[180] *Practice Note (CA: Crime: Applications for Leave to Appeal)* [1970] 1 WLR 663.

[181] *Monnell and Morris v United Kingdom (nos 9562/81 and 9818/82)* (1988) 10 EHRR 205 [30].

population may suggest that the Court of Appeal is in fact not overburdened with applications relative to what an appellate court may expect, but that if it has difficulty dealing with its caseload then other factors relevant to resourcing may be at play.

In *Monnell and Morris v United Kingdom*[182] the ECtHR found that loss of time orders can be compliant with the right to liberty (under Article 5 ECHR) and the right to a fair trial (under Article 6 of the ECHR). However, the ECtHR has not considered the question of the chilling effect on applicants of the fear of a loss of time order. In particular, it has not considered that a person may be deprived in practice of their right to appeal under Article 6 ECHR if they fear the negative consequences of the appeal. Even though the courts may have little sympathy for an applicant who advances a clearly unmeritorious case, the rights of all prospective appellants are potentially infringed by any chilling effect on the willingness to appeal.

Costs orders against applicants

Whether or not an applicant to the Court of Appeal is in custody, the Court of Appeal can consider making a costs order against them if they are unsuccessful.[183] Even if no costs have been incurred by a party to the case, the Court of Appeal can make a costs order to cover transcripts obtained by the Court of Appeal in considering the appeal.[184] Costs orders are extremely rare in practice, but the Court of Appeal has from time to time used cases to warn that they are available, even in cases where applicants are on benefits.[185]

---

182 *Monnell and Morris v United Kingdom (nos 9562/81 and 9818/82)* (n 181).

183 Prosecution of Offences Act 1985 s 18(2).

184 Prosecution of Offences Act 1985 s 18(6).

185 *Kirk, R v* [2015] EWCA Crim 1764.

Where an appellant in the Crown Court does not succeed on appeal, the prosecution will apply for their costs of the appeal, if they defended the appeal, currently £1,300.[186] The discretion to impose the costs lies with the Court, which will take into account the appellant's means, and may decide not to impose any costs at all.

Sanctions against lawyers

The Court of Appeal and the Crown Court can also make costs orders against lawyers.[187] Costs orders against lawyers in criminal appeals are very rare even in cases of proven failures to comply with lawyers' duties to the court. Where a costs sanction is considered, the Court of Appeal will usually choose the easier target of the applicant. Where lawyers are faced with the prospect of costs sanctions, they will generally be insured and represented. Barristers will almost inevitably have their representation in costs proceedings taken care of by the Bar Mutual Indemnity Fund and, due to the low deductible of their insurance, their personal financial exposure to any wasted costs order will tend to be very limited.[188] The costs and effort of recovering wasted costs against a lawyer may make considering making a wasted costs order unfeasible, and an ineffective deterrent against lawyers.

More common than a costs order is referral to a professional regulator. In this light, the importance of complying with the duty to ascertain the facts of the case from previous representatives was underlined in *Owusu Yianoma v Bar Standards Board*[189] in which the High Court found that a barrister's reckless failure to comply with his McCook duty justified his suspension from practice for 6 months.

---

[186] Crown Prosecution Service, 'Costs – Annex 1' (n 149).

[187] Prosecution of Offences Act 1985 s 19A.

[188] Bar Mutual Indemnity Fund, '2025 Terms of Cover'.

[189] *Owusu Yianoma v Bar Standards Board* [2023] EWHC 2785 (Admin).

CONCLUSION

In the introduction we explained that, over the last ten years, defences and appeals have become more accessible to victims of trafficking, including those who receive a conclusive grounds decision after their conviction.

However, the system for protecting victims of forced criminal exploitation remains woefully inadequate. We have seen individuals, particularly children and young people forced into dealing drugs, being criminalised as an alternative to protection. It often seems that criminalisation is the only way that the legal system knows how to deal with them. It is, overwhelmingly, vulnerable people who are exploited, and vulnerability is often linked to unstable housing. One young person who we were assisting on his criminal matters had for years asked the authorities to move him away from the area where he was being exploited. He was referred to a community care solicitor who successfully challenged the local authority's failure to relocate him away from the area where he was being repeatedly exploited. The successful challenge relied on legislation relating to children in need and care leavers as well as the protective duty under Article 4 ECHR. Criminal defence practitioners should be alive to those sorts of possibilities: only holistic legal challenges to failures to provide support to victims of trafficking can adequately protect such vulnerable people.

Many people are prosecuted while waiting to be investigated as victims of trafficking. That leaves a gap in the protections offered by Article 4 of the ECHR. Victims of trafficking are likely to be foreign nationals and so are likely to be denied bail; the way that decision-making is prioritised means that they will wait until very shortly before their trial date for a conclusive grounds decision.[190] That may mean six months or more in

[190] *R (on the application of FH) v Secretary of State for the Home Department* (n 54) paras 6, 87, 147, 154–158.

custody when they never should have been prosecuted at all. Taking into account the guidance given in *TV v Spain*[191] there may be scope for an argument that the requirement for the prosecution to wait for the conclusive grounds decision before deciding whether to continue prosecuting is causing Article 4 of the ECHR to be breached. If the prosecution and the police were required to seriously think for themselves about whether a person is a victim of trafficking, based on recognised trafficking indicators and the definition of trafficking, a significant proportion of prosecutions may fall to be discontinued *before* a conclusive grounds decision is made. This would reduce the number of people on remand in custody simply waiting for a conclusive grounds decision, only for that to be made, and prosecution discontinued immediately before trial. By that time the once-defendant now-victim will likely have been traumatised or retraumatised by an extended period of time in prison, and will be released without the benefit of the 30-day reflection and recovery period, which will have already passed while they were in custody.

Throughout their interaction with a case, criminal practitioners must remember that the right to non-punishment is not confined to issues of prosecution, conviction, and sentence. It extends to administrative and immigration penalties, and to the continuing effects of criminalisation. Full implementation of the right to non-punishment may require relief beyond an acquittal or a successful appeal, including expungement or sealing of criminal records and relief from associated sanctions.

Modern trafficking law originated with the UN Convention against Transnational Organised Crime, an instrument designed to criminalise traffickers. However, for practitioners interested in decriminalisation, the instruments and principles which flowed from it can provide a helpful tool. Although the principle that a victim of human trafficking or modern slavery should not face punishment for acts arising out of their victimisation is relatively straightforward, the implementation of that

---

[191] *TV v Spain (no. 22512/21)* (n 34).

principle remains uneven and contradictory across the criminal legal system. This is not helped by the quickly evolving regulations, statutory guidance, and caselaw. We hope that this book will help practitioners to navigate this area.

MORE BOOKS BY LAW BRIEF PUBLISHING

A selection of our other titles available now:-

'A Practical Guide to Probation Breaches and Other Applications' by Mark Thomas
'A Practical Guide to Remarriage and Divorce' by Cordelia Williams & Claire Howard
'A Practical Guide to Privacy, Transparency, Reporting Restrictions and Closed Proceedings in the Court of Protection' by Laura Mannering
'Beaumont on Barristers – A Guide to Defending Disciplinary Proceedings (Second Edition)' by Marc Beaumont
'A Practical Guide to Payments for Environmental Services' by Ben Sharples
'A Practical Guide to the Law of Pregnancy and Maternity at Work' by Rebecca Thomas
'A Practical Guide to Redundancy – Second Edition' by Philip Hyland & Collette Moore
'A Practical Guide to International Issues for Scottish Family Lawyers' by Susie Mountain, Donna McKay, Ken MacDonald
'A Practical Guide to the Law on Deprivation of Liberty' by Ben Troke
'A Practical Guide to Rights over Airspace and Subsoil – Second Edition' by Daniel Gatty
'A Practical Guide to the Law in Relation to Inquests' by Ramya Nagesh
'A Practical Guide to the Construction and Rectification of Wills and Trust Instruments (Second Edition)' by Edward Hewitt
'A Practical Guide to Data Protection in Social Housing' by Clare Paterson
'A Practical Guide to Spousal Maintenance – Second Edition' by Liz Cowell
'A Practical Guide to International Parental Child Abduction Law (England and Wales)' by Dr Onyója Momoh
'A Practical Guide to Deprivation of British Citizenship' by Sean Ell
'A Practical Guide to Commercial Property Service Charges' by Rachel Garton
'A Practical Guide to Clinical Negligence – Third Edition' by Geoffrey Simpson-Scott (Geoff)
'A Practical Guide to the Rights of Grandparents in Children Proceedings – Second Edition' by Stuart Barlow

'The Electronic Communications Code: A Practical Guide – Second Edition' by Kerry Bretherton KC, James Castle, Mark Loveday
'A Practical Guide to the Independent School Standards – September 2023 Edition' by Sarah McKimm
'A Practical Guide to Estate Administration and Crypto Assets' by Richard Marshall
'A Practical Guide to Parental Alienation in Private and Public Law Children Cases' by Sam King QC & Frankie Shama
'Contested Heritage – Removing Art from Land and Historic Buildings' by Richard Harwood QC, Catherine Dobson, David Sawtell
'The Limits of Separate Legal Personality: When Those Running a Company Can Be Held Personally Liable for Losses Caused to Third Parties Outside of the Company' by Dr Mike Wilkinson
'A Practical Guide to Transgender Law' by Robin Moira White & Nicola Newbegin
'A Practical Guide to 'Stranded Spouses' in Family Law' by Mani Singh Basi
'A Practical Guide to Residential Freehold Conveyancing' by Lorraine Richardson
'A Practical Guide to Pensions on Divorce for Lawyers' by Bryan Scant
'A Practical Guide to Challenging Sham Marriage Allegations in Immigration Law' by Priya Solanki
'A Practical Guide to Digital Communications Evidence in Criminal Law' by Sam Willis
'A Practical Guide to Legal Rights in Scotland' by Sarah-Jane Macdonald
'A Practical Guide to New Build Conveyancing' by Paul Sams & Rebecca East
'A Practical Guide to Inherited Wealth on Divorce' by Hayley Trim
'A Practical Guide to Practice Direction 12J and Domestic Abuse in Private Law Children Proceedings' by Rebecca Cross & Malvika Jaganmohan
'A Practical Guide to Confiscation and Restraint' by Narita Bahra QC, John Carl Townsend, David Winch
'A Practical Guide to the Law of Forests in Scotland' by Philip Buchan
'A Practical Guide to Health and Medical Cases in Immigration Law' by Rebecca Chapman & Miranda Butler
'A Practical Guide to Bad Character Evidence for Criminal Practitioners by Aparna Rao
'A Practical Guide to Extradition Law post-Brexit' by Myles Grandison et al
'A Practical Guide to Hoarding and Mental Health for Housing Lawyers' by Rachel Coyle

'Stephens on Contractual Indemnities' by Richard Stephens
'A Practical Guide to the EU Succession Regulation' by Richard Frimston
'A Practical Guide to Solicitor and Client Costs – Second Edition' by Robin Dunne
'Constructive Dismissal – Practice Pointers and Principles' by Benjimin Burgher
'A Practical Guide to Religion and Belief Discrimination Claims in the Workplace' by Kashif Ali
'A Practical Guide to the Law of Medical Treatment Decisions' by Ben Troke
'Fundamental Dishonesty and QOCS in Personal Injury Proceedings: Law and Practice' by Jake Rowley
'A Practical Guide to the Law in Relation to School Exclusions' by Charlotte Hadfield & Alice de Coverley
'A Practical Guide to Divorce for the Silver Separators' by Karin Walker
'The Right to be Forgotten – The Law and Practical Issues' by Melissa Stock
'A Practical Guide to Planning Law and Rights of Way in National Parks, the Broads and AONBs' by James Maurici QC, James Neill et al
'A Practical Guide to Election Law' by Tom Tabori
'A Practical Guide to the Law in Relation to Surrogacy' by Andrew Powell
'A Practical Guide to Claims Arising from Fatal Accidents – Second Edition' by James Patience
'A Practical Guide to Asbestos Claims' by Jonathan Owen & Gareth McAloon
'A Practical Guide to Stamp Duty Land Tax in England and Northern Ireland' by Suzanne O'Hara
'A Practical Guide to the Law of Farming Partnerships' by Philip Whitcomb
'A Practical Guide to the Law of Unlawful Eviction and Harassment – Second Edition' by Stephanie Lovegrove
'A Practical Guide to Costs in Personal Injury Claims – Second Edition' by Matthew Hoe
'A Practical Guide to the General Data Protection Regulation (GDPR) – Second Edition' by Keith Markham
'A Practical Guide to Working with Litigants in Person and McKenzie Friends in Family Cases' by Stuart Barlow
'Protecting Unregistered Brands: A Practical Guide to the Law of Passing Off' by Lorna Brazell
'A Practical Guide to Secondary Liability and Joint Enterprise Post-Jogee' by Joanne Cecil & James Mehigan

'A Practical Guide to the Pre-Action RTA Claims Protocol for Personal Injury Lawyers' by Antonia Ford
'A Practical Guide to Neighbour Disputes and the Law' by Alexander Walsh
'A Practical Guide to Coercive Control for Legal Practitioners and Victims' by Rachel Horman
'A Practical Guide to the Law of Driverless Cars – Second Edition'
by Alex Glassbrook, Emma Northey & Scarlett Milligan
'A Practical Guide to TOLATA Claims' by Greg Williams
'A Practical Guide to Elderly Law – Second Edition' by Justin Patten
'A Practical Guide to Responding to Housing Disrepair and Unfitness Claims' by Iain Wightwick
'A Practical Guide to the Law of Bullying and Harassment in the Workplace' by Philip Hyland
'How to Be a Freelance Solicitor: A Practical Guide to the SRA-Regulated Freelance Solicitor Model' by Paul Bennett
'A Practical Guide to Prison Injury Claims' by Malcolm Johnson
'A Practical Guide to Advising Clients at the Police Station' by Colin Stephen McKeown-Beaumont
'A Practical Guide to Antisocial Behaviour Injunctions – Second Edition' by Iain Wightwick
'Practical Mediation: A Guide for Mediators, Advocates, Advisers, Lawyers, and Students in Civil, Commercial, Business, Property, Workplace, and Employment Cases' by Jonathan Dingle with John Sephton
'The Mini-Pupillage Workbook' by David Boyle
'A Practical Guide to Crofting Law' by Brian Inkster
'A Practical Guide to the Law of Domain Names and Cybersquatting' by Andrew Clemson
'A Practical Guide to the Law of Gender Pay Gap Reporting' by Harini Iyengar
'NHS Whistleblowing and the Law' by Joseph England
'Employment Law and the Gig Economy' by Nigel Mackay & Annie Powell
'A Practical Guide to Noise Induced Hearing Loss (NIHL) Claims' by Andrew Mckie, Ian Skeate, Gareth McAloon
'An Introduction to Beauty Negligence Claims – A Practical Guide for the Personal Injury Practitioner' by Greg Almond
'Intercompany Agreements for Transfer Pricing Compliance' by Paul Sutton
'Zen and the Art of Mediation' by Martin Plowman
'A Practical Guide to Adoption for Family Lawyers' by Graham Pegg

'A Practical Guide to Industrial Disease Claims' by Andrew Mckie & Ian Skeate
'A Practical Guide to Conducting a Sheriff Court Proof' by Andrew Stevenson
'A Practical Guide to Vicarious Liability' by Mariel Irvine
'A Practical Guide to Applications for Landlord's Consent and Variation of Leases' by Mark Shelton
'A Practical Guide to Relief from Sanctions Post-Mitchell and Denton' by Peter Causton
'A Practical Guide to Equity Release for Advisors' by Paul Sams
'A Practical Guide to Financial Services Claims' by Chris Hegarty
'A Practical Guide to Financial Ombudsman Service Claims' by Adam Temple & Robert Scrivenor
'A Practical Guide to Running Housing Disrepair and Cavity Wall Claims – Second Edition' by Andrew Mckie & Ian Skeate
'A Practical Guide to Holiday Sickness Claims – Second Edition' by Andrew Mckie & Ian Skeate
'Arguments and Tactics for Personal Injury and Clinical Negligence Claims' by Dorian Williams
'A Practical Guide to Drone Law' by Rufus Ballaster, Andrew Firman, Eleanor Clot
'On Experts: CPR35 for Lawyers and Experts' by David Boyle
'An Introduction to Personal Injury Law' by David Boyle

www.ingramcontent.com/pod-product-compliance
Ingram Content Group UK Ltd.
Pitfield, Milton Keynes, MK11 3LW, UK
UKHW020146290926
15471UKWH00004B/716

9 781918 241204